The Role
of Women
in the
Church

CHARLES CALDWELL RYRIE

The Role
of Women
in the
Church

MOODY PRESS
CHICAGO

THE ROLE OF WOMEN IN THE CHURCH
formerly published as
THE PLACE OF WOMEN IN THE CHURCH

© *Charles Caldwell Ryrie 1958*

Library of Congress catalog card number: 58-8329

ISBN: 0-8024-7370-9

Moody Press Edition, 1970

Moody Paperback Edition, 1978

Second Printing, 1979

Printed in the United States of America

To my mother

PREFACE

Attitudes toward the place of women in the church are rapidly changing in our day. The material in this book is presented so that all might have a better perspective concerning this subject which is coming to the forefront of ecclesiastical thought and life. Although one may choose not to be guided by the lessons of Scripture and history, one cannot afford to be ignorant of them. While the author has convictions concerning this subject, it is certainly not a doctrinal hobby with him. It is sincerely hoped that this book will be received in the same spirit in which it is offered.

The research which forms the basis for this work was done during studies at the University of Edinburgh, and the author wishes to acknowledge with appreciation the counsel of Professors J. H. S. Burleigh and Matthew Black.

May the Spirit of God whose ministry it is to guide us into all the truth (John 16:13) find teachable minds and hearts in all who read these pages.

CHARLES C. RYRIE

CONTENTS

I. BACKGROUNDS 1

The status of women in ancient Greece 2
The status of women in ancient Rome 5
The status of women in Judaism 7
The status of women in private life 8
The status of women in public life 11

Part I

THE EFFECT OF THE LIFE OF OUR LORD
ON THE STATUS OF WOMEN

II. THE MOTHER OF OUR LORD 19

Events related to the birth of Jesus 19
Mary's public encounters with Jesus 21
Mary's position and significance 23

III. THE ATTITUDE OF JESUS TOWARD WOMEN 26

Appreciation of woman's spiritual capability 26
Appreciation of woman's intellectual capability 27
Appreciation of woman's ability to serve 30

IV. WOMEN AS MINISTERS TO JESUS 34

V. JESUS' TEACHING ON DIVORCE 40

The historical situation 40
The teaching of Jesus 41
The problem in Matthew's Gospel 43
Explanation based on the authority of the church 43

Explanation based on the evidence of source
criticism · 44
Explanation based on the authority of inspiration · 45
Conclusions · 48

Part II

THE PLACE OF WOMEN IN THE LIFE OF THE CHURCH DURING THE APOSTOLIC AGE

VI. WOMEN AND THE FOUNDING OF THE CHURCH · 53

VII. THE DOMESTIC STATUS OF WOMEN · 59
Marriage, celibacy, and related matters · 59
Husband-wife relationship · 66

VIII. THE PLACE OF WOMEN IN CHURCH LIFE · 70
Women in public worship · 71
The question of subordination · 72
The question of silence · 74
Widows · 81
Deaconesses · 85

Part III

THE STATUS OF WOMEN IN THE LIFE OF THE CHURCH DURING THE SECOND AND THIRD CENTURIES

IX. THE AGE OF THE APOSTOLIC FATHERS AND APOLOGISTS · 97
The Apostolic Fathers · 97
The Apologists · 101
The contrast between Christian women and heathen
women · 101
The teaching concerning marriage · 102
Non-Christian literature · 102

X. THE ALEXANDRIAN FATHERS · 105
Clement's views on the status of women · 106
Relation of female to male · 106

The status of women as seen in the marriage
relationship 108
The status of women in church relationships 109
Origen's views on the status of women 110

XI. THE AFRICAN FATHERS 113

Tertullian's life and times 113
Tertullian's views on the status of women 115
Relation of the sexes 115
Marriage and celibacy 116
Virgins 117
Widows 118
The public ministry of women 119
Cyprian's life and times 121
Cyprian's views on the status of women 122
The public ministry of women 122
Widows 122
Virgins 122

XII. THE THIRD CENTURY CHURCH ORDERS 126

The Apostolic Tradition 127
The Apostolic Church Order 129
The Syrian Didascalia 131
Conclusions 135

XIII. CONCLUSIONS 138

SUBJECT INDEX 149

SCRIPTURE INDEX 152

Chapter I

BACKGROUNDS

Numerous difficulties beset the treatment of a subject such as the one discussed in this book. Feminists and faddists are but two of them. Author and reader alike must be constantly on guard against trying to prove a particular pet point from the historical facts. And yet, few subjects are as important as this in church life, activity, and government. There is scarcely an ecclesiastical body which has not discussed the place and service of women within its group today, and those which have not discussed the matter officially are facing the problem unofficially and on the local level. What did the introduction of Christianity do for the status of women? What does the New Testament say concerning their place in the home and church? How did those who lived in the days following the writing of the New Testament interpret its doctrines about women? These are but a few of the questions for which this book attempts to discover answers. The approach is historical, and the Word of God is considered inspired and authoritative. We seek fact, not fancy; truth, not theory; instruction, not imagination concerning principles for today.

Although the subject of this book will not permit a full and complete discussion of the status of women outside the Christian church, it is obviously imperative to begin with a survey of their position in ancient Greece, Rome, and Judaism. This will provide the necessary background for the ensuing discussion and will help to show at the very outset what effect, if any, the environment in which Christianity developed had on its message and practice; that is to say, to what extent the status of women in Christianity was dependent upon or to what extent it differed from their status in Greek, Roman, and Jewish life.

THE STATUS OF WOMEN IN ANCIENT GREECE

By comparison, Greek women were accorded somewhat higher respect than women of other ancient pagan societies. Nevertheless, it is true that they were placed almost on the same level with the slave and were under the authority and control of their husbands both by custom and by law. Plato, of course, vigorously affirmed the equality of the sexes and the community of wives.[1] He speaks of "the natural partnership of the sexes," [2] and as a result of that belief holds that "women naturally share in all pursuits." [3] However, Plato's views were exceptional. Actually, the truer representative of Greek thought was Aristotle, who regarded the inferiority of women as inherent in the sex.[4] The love of *The Symposium* is homosexual love, and "it is assumed without argument that this alone is capable of satisfying a man's highest and noblest aspirations, and the love of man and woman, when it is mentioned at all, is spoken of as altogether inferior, a purely physical impulse whose sole object is the procreation of children." [5]

The rise of the City-State was an important factor which affected the status of women in Greece. Since the City-State was supreme, all individual wishes were subordinated to it. In Sparta, for instance, women were cultivated physically in order that they might be good mothers and produce sons who would be superior warriors. No thought, however, was taken for women after their days of childbearing were over, with the result that standards became very lax. The marriage tie could be dissolved by the husband without any scruple, form, or legal process. This importance of breeding warriors for the State gave the women of Sparta full liberty to show themselves in public in the performance of bodily exercises. However, it is necessary to emphasize again that this liberty "was not the result of a philosophic idea of the equality of the two sexes, but was founded on the desire of producing strong children by means of strengthening the body of the female." [6]

In Athens, likewise, the State was all important. All the citizens of Athens were connected by blood ties of some sort, and they took great pains to maintain this relationship. Consequently, careful distinction was made between citizens and strangers and between the offspring of each group. Citizen women, therefore, were forced to lead very secluded lives. Their existence is well described thus:

The life of married women, maidens, children while in the care of women, and of female slaves, passed in the gynaikonites [the part of the house reserved for domestic purposes], from which they issued only on rare occasions. The family life of Greek women widely differed from our Christian idea; neither did it resemble the life in an Oriental harem, to which it was far superior. The idea of the family was held up by both law and custom, and although concubinage and the intercourse with hetairai was suffered, nay favoured, by the State, still such impure elements never intruded on domestic relations. Our following remarks refer, of course, only to the better classes, the struggle for existence by the poor being the same in all ages. In the seclusion of the gynaikonites the maiden grew up in comparative ignorance. The care bestowed on domestic duties and on her dress was the only interest of her monotonous existence. Intellectual intercourse with the other sex was wanting entirely. Even where maidens appeared in public at religious ceremonies, they acted separately from the youths. . . . Even marriage did not change this state of things. The maiden only passed from the gynaikonites of her father into that of her husband. In the latter, however, she was the absolute ruler, the *oikodespoina* of her limited sphere. She did not share the intellectual life of her husband. . . . It is true that the husband watched over her honour with jealousy, assisted by gynaikonomoi, sometimes even by means of lock and key . . . her position was only that of the mother of the family. Indeed, her duties and achievements were hardly considered, by the husband, in a much higher light than those of a faithful domestic slave.[7]

Such seclusion, however, did not mean that these wives were ignorant women, for many were self-trained. Nonetheless, although the Greeks were a race of great thinkers, poets, sculptors, painters, and architects, "not one Athenian woman ever attained to the slightest distinction in any one department of literature, art, or science."[8] However, this seclusion did not mean inactivity, for the wife was in full charge of all domestic affairs of her household. She was absolute ruler in this realm, and in its own way it was a place of honor. But Pericles expresses the prevailing view concerning women in the funeral oration which Thucydides puts into his mouth:

If I am to speak also of womanly virtues . . . I will sum up all in a brief admonition: Great is your glory if you fall not below the standard which nature has set for your sex, and great also is hers of whom there is least talk among men whether in praise or in blame.[9]

The stranger women, called *hetairai,* did not, we may be sure, lead a monastic existence simply because they were forbidden to marry citizens. They enjoyed much greater freedom than the wives of citizens, and they became the companions, both intellectual and physical, of Athenian men. Demosthenes' summary of the status of these various groups of women is brutally frank: "Hetairai we keep for the sake of pleasure, concubines for the ordinary requirements of the body, wives to bear us legitimate children and to be faithful guardians of our households."[10]

After the time of Alexander the Great, women began to have a relatively greater measure of freedom. This was especially true in Macedonia, and was due largely to the fact that Macedonian dynasties produced an extraordinary succession of able and masterful women such as Arsinoë, Berenice, and Cleopatra. These women played a large part in civic affairs, for they "received envoys . . . built temples, founded cities, engaged mercenaries, commanded armies, held fortresses, and acted on occasion as regents or co-rulers."[11] What is more important is that from the courts of Macedonia came relative freedom to those women who desired emancipation. They could be educated, take part in club life, appear at the games, and in general enjoy freer relations with men. Nevertheless, "most of these things clearly relate only to a minority. Freedom was not automatic, but had to be grasped; education for the mass was rudimentary, and even in the first century there were women, rich enough to own slaves, who could neither read nor write. Greece suffered from the sexes being on different levels of culture." [12]

Thus we may conclude that in the Greek world the status of women was decidedly inferior to that of men; wives led lives of seclusion and practical slavery; the hetairai, though enjoying more freedom of movement at least, did not share the rights or status that belonged to men; and the relative freedom which did come to women in places like Macedonia was enjoyed only by a minority.

THE STATUS OF WOMEN IN ANCIENT ROME

Under the Roman Empire women enjoyed a somewhat better standing than in Greece. Legally, however, the wife was still regarded merely as a piece of property completely under the control of the husband. Yet in practice the law was interpreted otherwise, and women enjoyed considerable freedom. Further, the wife was not kept in seclusion as in a Greek household; rather, "she shared her husband's life and set a standard of wifely and motherly virtues envied in a later age." [13]

Any such freedom was not, of course, gained all at once. The laws of the Republic made every father and husband a despot, and because some husbands chose to act their legally constituted role there were two waves of feminine reaction which took the form of mass poisoning of husbands in 331 B.C. and 180 B.C. In 215 B.C. a law proposed by Oppius at a time when state finances were low and expenditures had to be curbed provided that "no woman should be allowed to possess more than a half ounce of gold, to wear a parti-colored garment, to ride in a chariot within the city of Rome or a town occupied by Roman citizens, or within a mile of these places, except for religious purposes." [14] When more prosperous days returned, Roman matrons, who had been chafing under this law, sought and won its repeal. One of the arguments against the repeal was this: "If they win in this, what will they not attempt? Review all the laws with which your forefathers restrained their license and made them subject to their husbands, even with all these bonds you can scarcely control them." [15] These quotations show clearly both the restraint under which Roman women lived (subject to their husbands) and the freedom which they enjoyed (being at liberty to appear in public).

Along with this partial emancipation came increased moral laxity. Women sought escape from the control of their husbands with the result that divorce became a more common thing. Though we need not believe that Seneca's famous remark about divorce represented the condition of the majority of women, it nonetheless indicates the trend of the day. He asked (in A.D. 54), "Is there any woman that blushes at divorce now that certain illustrious and noble ladies reckon their years, not by the number of consuls, but by the number of their husbands, and leave home in order to marry, and marry in order to be divorced?" [16] In addition, other vices were common in Roman society at the time of Christ. Another has summarized the situation well:

With rare exceptions, they [the Romans] copied only the vices of the Greeks. The old frugal, industrious, and virtuous manner of life practised by their ancestors was in too many instances exchanged for an idle, luxurious, and sensual existence. . . . Hand in hand with increasing wealth and outward prosperity came indolence and corruption, and the State whose citizens could boast that for five centuries no Roman had ever to divorce his wife, sank under the emperors to the pitch of moral degradation mirrored . . . in the opening chapter of Paul's epistle. The fountains of life were poisoned. Although the position of women in Rome was for long a much more dignified one than in Greece, there was latterly a greatly diminished value set on marriage, a marked increase in divorces, a general casting off of moral restraint. In the last pre-Christian century almost every vice was rampant—immorality and paiderastia, abortion and infanticide, gluttony and avarice, cruelty and sycophancy, gambling and suicide, indecency in pictures, at public races, and on the stage.[17]

Religious movements had both good and bad effects on the status of women. Stoicism, first taught in Greece by Zeno and taken over in Roman times by the philosopher Seneca, the slave Epictetus, and the emperor Marcus Aurelius, tended to elevate the position of women. It inculcated lofty ethical standards, including a single standard of chastity for men and women alike. On the other hand, the worship of Bacchus, which was practiced by many women, incorporated many shameful vices which greatly degraded women. In 181 B.C. the cult was declared illegal, and the worst offenders were put to death.[18]

Balance is the most necessary ingredient in trying to arrive at a true evaluation of the status of women in Roman society. It is not easy to avoid a one-sided exaggeration. The moral principles of Stoicism must be balanced with the knowledge that they were not widely applied; the evident degradation of society must be balanced with the realization that "among the common people throughout the empire there were doubtless many who had neither part nor lot in the ridiculous dainties or bestial practices of the wanton revellers pilloried in the literature of the age." [19] It is clear that women enjoyed greater practical, if not legal, freedom in Roman than in Greek society, and this aided the spread of Christianity because women participated more freely in religious activities. It also resulted in the laxity and licentiousness against which Christianity spoke and from which it protected its women. Finally, we may conclude that the most important relation between Christianity and the Roman way of life is a relation of contrast, and almost all agree that Christian teaching concerning women stood in sharp contrast to anything found in the heathen world.

THE STATUS OF WOMEN IN JUDAISM

A woman's position in Judaism seems to be a paradox. On the one hand there is the well known saying of the synagogue service,

"Blessed art thou, O Lord our God, King of the universe, who hast not made me a woman." [20] On the other hand there are the lofty words concerning womanhood in the Proverbs:

Who can find a virtuous woman? for her price is far above rubies. . . . Strength and honour are her clothing; and she shall rejoice in time to come. She openeth her mouth with wisdom; and in her tongue is the law of kindness. She looketh well to the ways of her household, and eateth not the bread of idleness. Her children arise up, and call her blessed; her husband also, and he praiseth her.[21]

The paradox can only be solved with a right understanding of woman's sphere of service, for "according to Jewish ideas, the special and supreme sphere of woman is the home. There her position has always been one of unchallenged dignity. Public affairs and public activities lie outside the home—and therefore outside woman's special sphere." [22] Even the prayer of the synagogue service quoted above supports this idea of a special sphere, for immediately following that prayer which is offered by the men is one offered by the women, who say, "Blessed art thou, O Lord our God, King of the universe, who hast made me according to thy will." [23] J. H. Hertz's commentary on its meaning asserts that the true spirit of it is: "who has made me a woman, to win hearts for thee by motherly love or wifely devotion; and to lead souls to thee, by daughter's care or sisterly tenderness and loyalty." [24] Thus these prayers, which were instituted after Ezra's revival, emphasize the distinction between the sexes and the special sphere of service of each.

It is true, however, that Judaism did share the universal conception of the inferiority of women; but it, unlike Mohammedanism, for instance, did not sanction the total subjection of women to men, but rather sought to elevate women in their proper sphere. Neither was there in Judaism the separation of the sexes so common among other peoples, for Hebrew women mixed more freely and often took a positive and influential part in both public and private affairs.

The status of women in private life. The distinctiveness and dignity of women are well illustrated in the private, family life in Israel. Immediately there come to mind outstanding women in Jewish history such as Sarah, Rebekah, Leah, Rachel (designated the "four mothers" by the Rabbis), as well as Manoah's wife, Hannah, Ruth, Naomi, and Esther, whose private lives played an important part in Israel's history.

Nevertheless, distinctiveness and inferiority were recognized at the birth of a female child, for the Jews required a double period of purification after the birth of a girl.[25] When it came time for the child to be educated, she would discover that the Rabbis disapproved of the same amount of instruction being given to her as to boys. Certain branches of learning, such as legal studies, were entirely forbidden to women simply because the Rabbis felt that a woman's mind was incapable of grasping such investigations. However, all this does not mean that the education of girls was entirely neglected. In the time of Christ, children of the poor were educated by means of contributions collected in the temple, and orphans were the special charge of the whole congregation.[26] Attendance at religious ceremonies further contributed to the education of girls, and it is evident from the New Testament accounts of such women as Lois, Eunice, and Priscilla that some Hebrew women obtained a good religious education. But, in general, it is true that there was little recognition of the mental capacities of women.

The paradoxical situation of subordination and dignity is further illustrated in matrimonial matters. Subordination is seen in the woman's legal rights, and dignity is evinced by her position and activity in the home. Legally, the position of a Jewish woman was very low. One writer declares that "it would be misleading to apply the term 'free-woman' to any Israelitess, except perhaps to a widow." [27] Female slaves were, of course, at the complete disposal of their masters. The concubine's position was slightly better because certain restrictions were imposed upon one who had a concubine. If he no longer desired her, he could not simply dismiss her but either had to maintain her, let her go free, or permit her relatives to redeem her.[28]

In reality, however, the Jewish woman occupied a more dignified

position than her legal status would suggest. Although polygamy
was permitted in Israel, there is no doubt that the monogamy of the
patriarchs was held up as the example to be followed. Certainly
the description of the virtuous woman in the Proverbs presupposes
monogamy. However, the right of divorce was at the discretion of
the husband, and all that the wife could expect was a bill of divorce-
ment.[29] In the days of Malachi divorce was quite common; [30] but by
the time that Christ appeared on earth it was probably much less
frequent, since in the first century B.C. it came to be required that
the dowry had to be returned if the wife was divorced.[31] It does
not follow, however, from these facts that Christianity inherited from
Judaism only a morally lax and legally rigid standard in matrimonial
matters. Doubtless there were many faithful women who "must
have kept the moral atmosphere pure and sweet, and shed precious
light on their homes and on society, corrupt to the core as it was
under the sway of heathenism." [32]

In the home the Jewish woman's position was one of dignity
and responsibility. She was her husband's conscience charged with
the task of encouraging him in all holiness.[33] Children, who were a
sign of the blessing of God on a home, were the special charge of
the mother. It seems to have been the general practice that the
mother named the children.[34] As the children grew older it became
the woman's holy vocation to assist in their training, for the first
teaching would naturally devolve on the mother. And yet in this
training she did not act alone, for the father joined her in a
coordinate relationship, and equal reverence to both parents was
expected from the children.[35] Thus in this regard, at least, a Jewish
mother fulfilling her responsibilities in the sphere of her home
receives equal honor with the father. Further evidence of the influence of the mother in the lives of her children is the attention
given to the naming of the mothers of the kings of Judah in the
Old Testament. The mother of Zebedee's children, the mother of
John Mark, women like Lois and Eunice also illustrate the influence of the mother. Judaism hallowed the home; both parents
ministered to the congregation of children. In this, Christianity has
drawn in large measure on its heritage in Judaism. Subordination,

subjection, dignity, and responsibility correctly describe the various aspects of the private life of a Hebrew woman, but in the sphere of the home her place was beyond question a prominent one.

The status of women in public life. For a Jewish woman public life is practically synonymous with religious life, and in this her role was neither passive nor one of leadership. The religious feeling which she possessed in common with others was bound to assert itself, as it did in various ways. Basic to all this is the fact that "all the people," [36] including women, were part of God's covenant relationship which He introduced through Moses. That women were surely a part of this relationship is made clear by the special protecting commandments given concerning them.[37] Very few even notice this point, but one at least has correctly observed that "that which distinguishes the God of Israel from the gods of the nations is, among other traits, his condescension to the humble; he deigns to establish his covenant with the children, the women and the slaves." [38] Since we believe that Judaism was a supernaturally given religious revelation from God, this point gains importance, for it guarantees women a standing before the true God which they did not have in any heathen religious relationship.

Although the position was thus, the practice was not, for "the majority of women were entirely dependent on man, and became in religious matters a sort of appendix to their husbands, who by their good actions insured salvation also for them." [39] Nevertheless, there is sufficient evidence of distinctively feminine religious activities to enable one to see that women did make some use of their privilege as co-heirs of the covenant.

The Mosaic Law expected the presence of women at the sanctuary at the festal seasons, for daughters and maidservants were to join with sons and manservants.[40] Women were present in the congregation when the Law was read in the time of Nehemiah. Likewise, they were at the feast which David made in honor of the recovering of the ark,[41] and the daughters of Shiloh could be counted on to be present at the annual feast.[42] Hannah and Peninnah who went yearly to the gathering in Shiloh are examples of women participating in public prayer.[43] Furthermore, women could take

part in the sacrifices, for the fact that they were forbidden to eat
the flesh of the sin offering indicates that they were permitted to
share in other offerings,[44] and there is no question but that they
offered sacrifices for purification.[45] Women, as well as men, were
permitted to separate themselves unto Jehovah by taking the vow of
a Nazarite.[46] Theophanies were not the experience of men only,
for there are records of God or the messenger of God appearing to
Eve,[47] Hagar,[48] Sarah,[49] and the mother of Samson.[50] In addition,
rites of mourning were performed by men and women and for men
and women alike.[51] Although a prophetess was an exceptional thing,
several outstanding ones appeared in Israel. Miriam, who is called
a prophetess, shared eminence with her brothers Moses and Aaron.[52]
Deborah was a prophetess as well as a judge,[53] and Huldah the
prophetess was an authority in the days of Josiah whom the king
and the high priest could consult in a matter of spiritual interpretation.[54] Mention is also made of a prophetess in Isaiah,[55] of the
prophetess Noadiah,[56] and the aged Anna who was present at
Jesus' circumcision.[57]

In several instances one of the gifts of the prophetesses was the
utterance of inspired songs. More commonly, however, singing
women, as well as men, were attached to the temple and helped
form a temple choir.[58] Ewald thinks, on the basis of Psalm 68:24–25,
that these women also lived at the temple, but in any case it is
certain that we may not ascribe to them any sacerdotal functions.[59]
It is also recorded that women danced on occasions of great victory.

The earliest allusion to women's participating in public worship
is the reference to the serving women at the door of the tabernacle.[60]
The Hebrew word *tsabbath* suggests a sort of guard of honor
around the sanctuary, but further than that it is impossible to say
what the work of these women might have been. In the days of
the synagogue when the practice was to invite anyone to speak who
had something to say to the edification of the people, there is no
record of any woman ever addressing the synagogue.[61] However,
titles of honor were conferred on women, such as "Mistress of the
Synagogue," "Mother of the Synagogue," and even "Ruler of the
Synagogue." Although the corresponding office to these titles was

not common until after the time of Christ, it seems likely that the title was bestowed during the years of His life. However, the office did not carry with it any ministerial or liturgical duties, and the titles were simply titles of honor given to "meritorious work connected with a religious institution, viz., Charity," [62] because of the woman's "rank in the community" and "social weight." [63]

Thus, to say that the role of Jewish women in the public religious life of Israel was solely a passive one would not be accurate. To them belonged certain religious privileges under the covenant which heathen women did not enjoy. Many religious activities were open to them, and some women participated in them. Nevertheless, other activities were forbidden them, and one could not conclude that there was universal participation even in those activities open to them. Certainly they did not take a place of leadership as a general rule; rather, men dominated the public scene in Israel.

The major contribution of Jewish women was in their service in the home. Although their legal rights were practically non-existent, they were accorded a place of honor in carrying out the privileges of motherhood. The general principle which applied to the status of women in Judaism was, "The King's daughter *within the palace* is all glorious (Psalm xlv. 14), but *not* outside of it." [64]

It is evident from this survey that the teachings of Christianity concerning women bear many resemblances to those of Judaism. Equally clear is the fact that Christianity stands in sharp contrast to the treatment of women in ancient Greece and Rome. All of this will be demonstrated in greater detail as we proceed with the investigation of the status of women in the Christian church; meanwhile the purpose of this chapter—to sketch the situation into which the gospel came—has been fulfilled.

QUESTIONS

1. What sort of existence did the wife lead in a home in ancient Greece?
2. How did the religious life of Rome affect the women of that society?
3. What responsibilities did a Jewish mother have in her home?
4. Did a Jewish woman take any part in the religious life of the nation?

NOTES

[1] *The Republic*, V, V, 457–466.

[2] *Ibid.*, V, V, 466.

[3] *Ibid.*, V, V, 455.

[4] *Politics*, I, V, 2.

[5] W. Hamilton, translator, *The Symposium* (Harmondsworth, Penguin Books, 1951), p. 12.

[6] E. Guhl and W. Koner, *The Life of the Greeks and Romans* (London, Chapman & Hall, 1875), p. 186.

[7] *Ibid.*, p. 185.

[8] James Donaldson, *Woman: Her Position and Influence in Ancient Greece and Rome, and Among the Early Christians* (London, Longmans, Green & Co., 1874), p. 55.

[9] Thucydides, II, XLV, 2.

[10] *Theomnestus and Apollodorus Against Neaera*, 122.

[11] W. W. Tarn, *Hellenistic Civilization* (London, Edward Arnold & Co., 1927), p. 84.

[12] *Ibid.*, p. 86.

[13] R. H. Barrow, *The Romans* (Harmondsworth, Penguin Books, 1949), p. 21.

[14] Livy, XXXIV, I, 3.

[15] *Ibid.*, XXXIV, III, 1.

[16] Seneca, *De Beneficiis*, III, XVI, 2.

[17] William Fairweather, *The Background of the Epistles* (Edinburgh, T. & T. Clark, 1935), pp. 29–30.

[18] Livy, XXXIX, VIII.

[19] Fairweather, *op. cit.*, p. 29.

[20] *The Authorised Daily Prayer Book* (London, Shapiro, Valentine & Co., 1947), p. 21.

[21] Proverbs 31:10, 25–28.

[22] W. O. E. Oesterley and G. H. Box, *The Religion and Worship of the Synagogue* (London, Sir Isaac Pittman & Sons, 1907), pp. 297–298.

[23] *The Authorised Daily Prayer Book*, p. 21.

[24] *Loc. cit.*

[25] Leviticus 12:2, 5.

[26] Alfred Edersheim, *Sketches of Jewish Social Life in the Days of Christ* (London, Religious Tract Society, 1876), pp. 132–133.

[27] W. H. Bennett, "Family," *A Dictionary of the Bible*, I, 847.

[28] Exodus 21:7–11.

[29] Deuteronomy 24:1; Isaiah 50:1; Jeremiah 3:8.

[30] Malachi 2:16.

[31] George Foot Moore, *Judaism* (Cambridge, Harvard University Press, 1927), II, 123.

[32] Edersheim, *op. cit.*, p. 159.

[33] In the case of the ruler of the synagogue, it was deemed best that he be married, especially if he offered up prayer in the congregation, because his wife would preserve him from sin. Cf. Joshua L. Bernard, *The Synagogue and the Church* (London, B. Fellows, 1842), p. 148.

[34] Out of the 44 instances in which the naming of children is mentioned in the Old Testament, in 26 it is ascribed to women, in 14 to men, and in 4 to

God. Cf. Ismar J. Peritz, *Woman in the Ancient Hebrew Cult* (New York, Society of Biblical Literature and Exegesis, 1898), pp. 130–131.

[35] Exodus 20:12; 21:15, 17; Leviticus 19:3; Deuteronomy 5:16; Proverbs 1:8; 6:20; 20:20; 23:22; 28:24; 30:11, 17.

[36] Exodus 19:11.

[37] Exodus 22:22–24; Deuteronomy 22:13–30.

[38] H. Leclercq, "Femme," *Dictionnaire d'Archéologie Chrétienne et de Liturgie*, p. 1301.

[39] S. Schechter, *Studies in Judaism* (London, Adam & Charles Black, 1896), I, 388.

[40] Deuteronomy 12:12, 18; 14:26; 16:11, 14.

[41] II Samuel 6:19.

[42] Judges 21:6–25.

[43] I Samuel 1:1 ff.; 2:19 ff.

[44] Leviticus 6:29; 10:14.

[45] Leviticus 12; 15:19–33; Judges 13:20; Nehemiah 12:43.

[46] Numbers 6:2.

[47] Genesis 3:13 ff.

[48] Genesis 16:8 ff.; 21:17 ff.

[49] Genesis 18:9, 15.

[50] Judges 13:3 ff.

[51] Judges 11:40; II Chronicles 35:25; Jeremiah 16:7.

[52] Exodus 15:20; Numbers 12:2; Micah 6:4.

[53] Judges 4:4.

[54] II Kings 22:13–20.

[55] Isaiah 8:3.

[56] Nehemiah 6:14.

[57] Luke 2:36.

[58] Ezra 2:65; Nehemiah 7:67.

[59] Heinrich Ewald, *The History of Israel* (London, Longmans, Green & Co., 1878), p. 285.

[60] Exodus 38:8.

[61] Cf. Luke 4:16, 20; Acts 13:14 ff.

[62] Schechter, *op. cit.*, I, 386–387.

[63] Solomon Reinach, "Inscription Grecque de Smyrne. La Juive Rufina," *Revue des Etudes Juives*, VII, 165. Further references to the *archisunagōgos* will be found in Emil Schürer, *A History of the Jewish People in the Time of Jesus Christ* (Edinburgh, T. & T. Clark, 1885), II, 63–65; Vitringa, *De Synagoga Vetere* (Franequerae, J. Gyzelaar, 1696), pp. 580–592, 695–711; and W. M. Ramsay, *The Church in the Roman Empire* (London, Hodder & Stoughton, 1904), p. 480n.

[64] Schechter, *op. cit.*, I, 391.

PART I

The Effect of the Life of Our Lord on the Status of Women

Chapter II

THE MOTHER OF OUR LORD

Any study of the effect of the life and ministry of the Lord Jesus on the status of women must begin with a consideration of Mary His mother, for in a very real sense she marks the turning point in the history of women.

EVENTS RELATED TO THE BIRTH OF JESUS

Every pious Jewish woman hoped that she might be the mother of the Messiah, and in Mary that hope was realized. Two evangelists, Matthew and Luke, record the genealogy of Christ, Matthew prefacing his to the account of the beginning of Christ's life, and Luke his to the account of the beginning of His ministry.[1] It is at once apparent that there are differences in the two genealogies involving a number of problems not easily solved. Plummer says:

The difference between the two genealogies was from very early times felt to be a difficulty . . . and it is probable that so obvious a solution, as that one was the pedigree of Joseph and the other the pedigree of Mary, would have been very soon advocated, if there had been any reason (excepting the difficulty) for adopting it. But this solution is not suggested by anyone until Annius of Viterbo propounded it, *c.* A.D. 1490. . . . If we were in possession of all the facts, we might find that both pedigrees are in accordance with them.[2]

In spite of these difficulties, certain facts relevant to this discussion are clear; namely, in these genealogies are seen principles

of subordination and exaltation of women. Subordination is evident
in the legal position accorded to Mary. Matthew's intention in including the genealogy in his gospel was "to show that in Jesus, as
the heir of David and of Abraham, were fulfilled the promises made
to them: the pedigree itself is intended to illustrate this, rather
than to prove it, and it is not easy to avoid the conclusion that it is
quite artificial. . . ." [3] However, in order to demonstrate Jesus' right
to be heir of David and Abraham, Matthew has to stress the fact
that Joseph is the husband of Mary so that he may show that as
Joseph "recognized his wife's son in a *legal* sense his own, Jesus was
legally the heir of David." [4] Luke, of course, entirely omits Mary's
name, and while he is careful to avoid the impression that Jesus
might be merely the natural son of Joseph he also disallows the
possibility of slighting Jesus' kingly claims by avoiding linking Him
solely to His mother. [5] Thus, the subordination of women is evident again in Mary's having to be linked with the name of a man
in order to give legal status to her Son.

On the other hand, a singular exaltation of women is seen in
Matthew's genealogy in that he includes the names of four women:
Tamar, Rahab and Ruth, and Bathsheba. [6] This becomes especially
significant in a list that is selective as Matthew's is. It clearly shows
God's acceptance of woman's person, the extending of His forgive-
ness to them, and His receiving of them into the very line of the
Messiah. It is another way in which the world was prepared for
the teachings of Him who came in the fullness of time.

Turning from the genealogies, it is necessary to note one thing
in the annunciation—the angel's proclamation that Mary was "highly
favoured." [7] The verb used, *charitoō*, is found elsewhere in the New
Testament only in Ephesians 1:6, and from this latter passage "and
the analogy of verbs ending in *oō*, *kecharitōmenē* must mean 'en-
dued with grace.'" [8] Although great grace was bestowed upon Mary,
it was no greater than that which is bestowed upon every believer
today whether male or female.

When Mary returned to Nazareth after visiting Elizabeth, Joseph,
finding her with child, was minded to put her away privily. [9] Although Joseph was only espoused to Mary, this was entirely in order,

for "from the moment of her betrothal a woman was treated as if she were actually married. The union could not be dissolved, except by regular divorce; breach of faithfulness was regarded as adultery." [10] Making a public example of her "alludes to the law of the woman suspected of adultery set forth in the Book of Numbers V, 11–31." [11] But, of course, the appearance of the angel to Joseph solved his dilemma.[12]

All of these instances demonstrate two things: in many respects Mary is not an exceptional case, living as she did under Jewish customs regarding women in her day; and yet she is exceptional by virtue of her relationship to the Lord Jesus, and in this she is the turning point in the history of women by being the first fruits of that which the teachings of Jesus did for women. One further observation must be made: not only is her blessedness related to her Son, it is also related to motherhood. It is the obvious truth of saying that no man could have been the mother of Jesus, and yet it is so obvious that it is often overlooked. She is not only the mother *of our Lord;* she is the *Mother* of our Lord. The Mother could only be a woman; yet the Incarnation was in a man.

MARY'S PUBLIC ENCOUNTERS WITH JESUS

Four times the general silence which surrounds Jesus' relationships with His mother is broken. The first is the time when He went to Jerusalem for the Passover at the age of twelve.[13] When Joseph and Mary missed the boy on the homeward journey and returned to find Him in the temple, He plainly told them that He must be about His Father's business. This strange and unexpected reply made it clear that in connection with the work which His Father had given Him to do there must be no interference from His mother. And yet the gospel writer adds that Jesus was subject to His parents. Here is an illustration of the later Pauline principle that obedience "in the Lord" is expected of children toward their parents.[14] As mothers, women are expected to fill a place of authority and leadership in relation to their children, but never to the compromising of the spiritual responsibilities of those children.

The second incident, the scene at the wedding in Cana, illustrates the same principle.[15] Here Mary appears without Joseph; indeed, this and "all the later notices of the Lord's Mother . . . confirm the supposition that he died before the Ministry began." [16] When the wine was used up, Mary appealed to Jesus for help, and He replied, "Woman, what have I to do with thee? mine hour is not yet come." There is no doubt that "Woman" is an address of respect,[17] but "what have I to do with thee" wherever used "marks some divergence between the thoughts and ways of the persons so brought together." [18] In this passage it "serves to show that the actions of the Son of God, now that He has entered on His divine work, are no longer dependent in any way on the suggestion of a woman, even though that woman be His Mother. . . . The time of silent discipline and obedience . . . was over." [19]

Anxiety must have prompted the third incident when Mary sought Jesus amid a crowd of people to whom He was ministering. When told that His mother and brothers were asking for Him, Jesus replied: "Behold my mother and my brethren! For whosoever shall do the will of God, the same is my brother, and my sister, and mother." [20] Swete summarizes well the significance of this remark:

This relative renunciation of kinship appears at the outset of the Ministry (Jo. ii. 4) and continues to the end (Jo. xix. 26), and a similar attitude is urged upon the disciples (Mc. x. 29). But it is a relative attitude only (Mt. x. 37), and is perfectly consistent with tender care for kinsmen, as the saying on the Cross shews . . . The bond which unites the family of God is obedience to the Divine Will.[21]

Again the incident illustrates the principle that supernatural relations transcend natural ones.[22]

Nevertheless, natural relationships and responsibilities are not obliterated, and the fourth encounter illustrates that. It is the incident at the cross where Mary is committed into John's keeping. "The Oriental, even the Jewish, mother would have been prostrate, with dishevelled hair and garments; Mary is found 'standing' (Jn 19:25). There is no mention of words, not even of tears. Silently and quietly at the direction of her Son she leaves the cross, though we know that a sword was at the time piercing her through and through." [23]

As far as the gospel records are concerned, there are no other recorded encounters of Mary with her Son. There is not even any record of a post-resurrection appearance to Mary, and however significant or embarrassing this may be in other respects, it is not important to this subject because our Lord did appear to other women after His resurrection. The importance of this will be discussed below.

MARY'S POSITION AND SIGNIFICANCE

A summary of what has been said concerning Mary is in order, partly to justify why so much space has been devoted to her. The incidents which involve her introduce and illustrate a number of themes which are further developed throughout the New Testament. The inclusion of women in the genealogy of Christ as a sign of God's favor; the emphasis on the blessing of Motherhood; the responsibility of a mother in the training of her child; the further, and often more difficult, responsibility of not standing in the way of that child's spiritual obligations and calling; the duty of children to their parents—themes which are developed elsewhere in the New Testament—are all illustrated by Mary's position in the gospels. That most of these are related to the home leads one to the conclusion that Mary is significant as a model of ideal Christian womanhood. There is certainly a dearth of material concerning Mary in the inspired text, and although this has been taken by some to be "a deliberate design on the part of the evangelists to reduce the mother to relative insignificance in the presence of her Divine Son," [24] one feels that the truer explanation is that "this slightness of texture is itself a note of genuine portraiture; for the reason that Mary was of a retiring nature, unobtrusive, reticent, perhaps even shrinking from observation, so that the impress of her personality was confined to the sweet sanctities of the home circle." [25] Or, as Walpole puts it, ". . . we see in the little that is told of her what a true woman ought to be." [26]

Finally, what were Mary's position and significance in the early church? The only other reference to her in the New Testament occurs in mentioning her among those gathered in the upper room before Pentecost.[27] After this her name disappears from the record, and even in the one instance she is not mentioned as any sort of fount of information concerning the Saviour nor does she take any place of leadership with or among the disciples. Ramsay has suggested that Mary or someone very close to her supplied Luke with the facts for his gospel; if this suggestion be true, then she did contribute, but not in any public way, to the life of the early church.[28]

QUESTIONS

1. What four women are included in the genealogy of Christ?

2. What are the four recorded occasions when Jesus encountered His mother in public?

3. Where is the last mention of the Virgin Mary in the Bible?

NOTES

[1] Matthew 1:1-17; Luke 3:23-38.

[2] Alfred Plummer, *A Critical and Exegetical Commentary on the Gospel According to St. Luke* (New York, Charles Scribner's Sons, 1900), p. 103.

[3] P. M. Bernard, "Genealogies of Jesus Christ," *A Dictionary of Christ and the Gospels*, I, 637.

[4] *Loc. cit.*

[5] This is true whether one understands the genealogy to be that of Joseph or of Mary; if the former, Jesus is linked to Joseph and the case is the same as in Matthew; if the latter, Jesus is linked to His grandfather Ḥeli through Mary but without mentioning her name, for the Jews said, *"Genuṣ matris non vacatur genus"* (*Baba bathra*, 110a). Roman Catholics generally hold the latter view (cf. A. J. Maas, "Virgin Mary," *The Catholic Encyclopedia*, XV, 464E. For a Protestant who holds it cf. F. Godet, *A Commentary on the Gospel of St. Luke* (Edinburgh, T. & T. Clark, 1890), I, 195-204.

[6] Matthew 1:3, 5, 6.

[7] Luke 1:28.

[8] Plummer, *op. cit.*, p. 22.

[9] Matthew 1:19.

[10] Edersheim, *Sketches* . . . , p. 148.

[11] David Werner Amram, *The Jewish Law of Divorce* (London, D. Nutt, 1897), p. 35n.

[12] Matthew 1:20.

[13] Luke 2:41-52.

[14] Ephesians 6:1.

[15] John 2:1-12.

[16] Henry Barclay Swete, *The Gospel According to St. Mark* (London, Macmillan, 1913), p. 112. Swete adds, "The Arabic *Historia Josephi* (cc. 14,

15) places his death in our Lord's eighteenth year, when Joseph had reached the age of 111."

[17] Cf. John 4:21; 19:26; 20:13, 15; Homer, *Iliad,* III, 204; Xenophon, *Cyropaedia,* V, i, 6.

[18] Brooke Foss Westcott, *The Gospel According to St. John* (London, John Murray, 1908), I, 82.

[19] *Loc. cit.*

[20] Mark 3:31–35.

[21] Swete, *op. cit.,* pp. 69–71.

[22] Cf. the incident in Luke 11:27–28.

[23] G. H. S. Walpole, "Woman," *A Dictionary of Christ and the Gospels,* II, 835.

[24] Walter F. Adeney, *Women of the New Testament* (London, James Nisbet & Co., 1901), p. 1.

[25] James Hastings, editor, *The Greater Men and Women of the Bible* (Edinburgh, 1915), V, 5.

[26] Walpole, *op. cit.,* II, 835.

[27] Acts 1:14.

[28] W. M. Ramsay, *Was Christ Born at Bethlehem?* (London, Hodder & Stoughton, 1898), p. 88. He says that the intermediary "is more likely to have been a woman than a man. There is a womanly spirit in the whole narrative, which seems inconsistent with the transmission from man to man. . . ."

Chapter III

THE ATTITUDE OF JESUS TOWARD WOMEN

Opinions vary concerning the interpretation of the attitude of our Lord toward women as shown in the gospels. Bishop Lightfoot comments that "to contemporaries it must have appeared in the light of a social revolution," [1] while Donaldson goes to the opposite extreme by stating emphatically that "an examination of the facts seems to me to show that there was no sign of this revolution in the first three centuries of the Christian era, and that the position of women among Christians was lower, and the notions in regard to them were more degraded than they were in the first." [2]

Speaking in general terms, it may be said that the gospels picture Christ as having an attitude of appreciating the distinct capabilities of women as personalities in their own right. Allworthy has well said that each individual gospel writer records "the powerful impression produced upon women by the personality and teaching of Jesus. This impression could only have been made by one who had a sincere belief in the intellectual and spiritual possibilities of women." [3] The truth of this statement will be demonstrated in this chapter.

APPRECIATION OF WOMAN'S SPIRITUAL CAPABILITY

The gospel counterpart to the Pauline statement that in Christ there is neither male nor female [4] is the Lord's saying that "whosoever shall do the will of God, the same is my brother, and my sister, and mother." [5] Early in His ministry, then, Jesus opened the doors to intimate affinity with Himself, and sex constituted no barrier to this intimacy. This was without any doubt so new that it may be

26

called a revolutionary saying, for "the story . . . has no Rabbinic ring." [6] In the same vein, Christ also said that His claims might set "the mother against the daughter, and the daughter against the mother; the mother-in-law against her daughter-in-law, and the daughter-in-law against her mother-in-law." [7] Although one must not read into this statement feminine equality with or superiority over men, still it may be said that it shows that "women might take an independent line in religion." [8]

There are two accounts in the gospels of Jesus' recognizing, honoring, and rewarding with physical healing the faith of women. One concerns a Jewish woman whose faith (though it may have been mixed with the superstition that Christ's garments could heal apart from His will) made her free from an issue of blood that had plagued her.[9] The other incident involved a Gentile woman; [10] and although this Syrophoenician was reminded by Jesus of the exclusiveness of the Jews in relation to the Gentiles, and although she was refused with sharpness,[11] her persistent faith was rewarded by the delivering of her daughter from an unclean spirit. These two events illustrate the capability of women in matters of recognized active faith as well as the appreciation of women on the part of Jesus which obliterated the barriers of sex and race.

APPRECIATION OF WOMAN'S INTELLECTUAL CAPABILITY

We have noted the unwillingness of the Rabbis to teach women, because education, except for that which could be given girls in the home, was for men only. But in the ministry of Jesus there is abundant evidence that He taught women privately, and there is every indication that, as part of the multitudes which followed Him, women heard His public teaching. The miracle of the feeding of the five thousand specifically states that there were women present in the crowd that followed the Master on that occasion, for Matthew expressly says so,[12] and the use of *anēr, male,* by the other writers clearly implies it. Further evidence that women were present in the crowds that heard the Lord's teaching is the interesting use He made of women in His parables and illustrations. For instance, the parable of the mustard seed which a *man* took and planted is followed by the parable of the leaven which a *woman* took and hid in the meal.[13] Though the parables teach different truths, it is not at all unlikely that our Lord varied the figure in order to capture the attention of men *and* women who were in the "great multitudes" that gathered on that occasion.[14]

The same phenomenon is repeated in another pair of parables recorded in Luke 15. The Lord speaks first of the joy of a *man* on finding a lost sheep (vv. 3–7) and then of the joy of a *woman* who found a lost coin (vv. 8–10). There can be no question that the main point of these parables is that "each sinner is so precious that God and His Ministers regard no efforts too great to reclaim such." [15] The same writer further suggests that the use of a woman's experience in the second parable shows that "woman also may work for the recovery of sinners." [16]

To illustrate the point further, other examples may be cited. To illustrate His teaching concerning prayer, the Lord spoke of an importunate friend who came asking food at midnight and of an importunate widow.[17] To teach His followers peace of mind He pointed to the lilies of the field which do not toil (man's work) or spin (woman's work).[18] To prepare them for His second coming to earth, He told His disciples that when it occurs one (*eis*) of two men in the field and one (*mia*) of two women grinding would be taken and the others left.[19] Admittedly it would be impossible to prove that women were actually present on each occasion cited (though it is clear that they were in the crowds who heard Jesus' public teaching in some of these instances); nevertheless there can be no doubt that the use our Lord makes of women in these parables and illustrations "is in fact evidence of His special interest in them." [20]

In addition to this public ministry, our Lord taught women individually and in private. Indeed, some of the most profound revelations concerning Himself and His Father were given in these instances. That He even did such a thing indicates His appreciation not only of the intellectual capacity in women but also of their spiritual capabilities.

The first of these instances took place on the Lord's journey from Judea to Galilee when he passed through Samaria.[21] While sitting at Jacob's well, and while the disciples were in the town buying food, He held a long theological discussion with a Samaritan harlot. The Rabbis had said that a man should not salute a woman, not even his own wife, in a public place,[22] but this dictum was probably not rigidly followed else we might expect that the Pharisees would have accused Jesus about this more often.[23] To talk to her may not have been contrary to the ordinary practice of the day, but to teach her certainly was. To hold this sort of conversation with a Samaritan, with whom the Jews had no dealing, was to break all convention and demonstrates Jesus' wider interest in people outside Judaism. That He should deal with a harlot shows His compassion and interest in the neediest of human beings. It is rightly said that "in this combination of freedom and pity . . . he makes a new departure of enormous significance and importance." [24] The entire scene was "a strange innovation on Rabbinic custom and dignity"; [25] and even those who may not admit the historical accuracy of the gospels must admit that since there is no evident theological reason for inserting a female person into this story there must be a historical basis. In the conversation the Lord spoke of the deep truths of living water and proper worship; and although there is no command from Christ to this woman to testify of what she had been taught, He did not disapprove of or reject the witness which she bore and which resulted in bringing many men to Him. Women, indeed, may work for the reclamation of sinners.

On many occasions the Lord Jesus visited the house of Mary, Martha, and Lazarus in Bethany. On the very first recorded visit [26] He is seen teaching Mary who "sat at Jesus' feet, and heard his word." After a bit Martha, who was distracted with much serving and who "could not think that a woman could, in such manner [as Mary's], fulfil her duty, or show forth her religious profiting," [27] complains that her sister should also be helping with the domestic preparations. Our Lord in reply taught her with gentle reproof and yet with affection that "one thing is needful"; that is, the care of the spiritual life.

Later in Christ's ministry, Lazarus, one of the members of

this home, died.[28] When Jesus appeared at Bethany four days after Lazarus' death, He revealed to the two sisters the profound truth that Resurrection and Life are the outcome of His very being. Since resurrection at the end of time was part of the religious hope of every Jew, Martha doubtless thought that Jesus' first words to her— "Thy brother shall rise again"—were nothing more than the accustomed consolation. But our Lord reveals to her that "the Resurrection of the Dead is no longer bound up purely or primarily with an historical event at the end of time, but connects immediately with the Person of Jesus Christ and with the life which He bestows here and now." [29]

Of course, one must remember that most of the Lord's teaching was to men and especially to His twelve disciples, but these instances cited are ample proof of His revolutionary recognition of women, His confidence in their capabilities, and His concern for their spiritual education and welfare.

APPRECIATION OF WOMAN'S ABILITY TO SERVE

Other accounts in the gospels give indication of the kind of service Jesus received and appreciated from women. On one occasion He used a woman to teach some religious leaders the grace of forgiveness in mixing mercy with law, and although this incident recorded in John 8:2-11 is poorly attested, it nonetheless probably relates a historic event.[30] Similarly, on another occasion the sacrificial giving of a widow was used to teach the disciples that true value is based not on quantity but on quality.[31] In other words, our Lord held up to men the lives and examples of women.

On at least two occasions Jesus received the public testimony of women. While teaching in a synagogue on the Sabbath, He called, as if deliberately, a woman to Him and healed her of her infirmity. She immediately glorified God so as to bring an indignant rebuke from the ruler of the synagogue but not from the Master.[32] In the other instance, the healing of the woman who touched the hem of His garment, Christ called for the public declaration of her faith. No doubt this was done "to bring her to clearness in the exercise of her faith," [33] but in so doing the woman gave her testimony "before all the people." [34]

On two other occasions Jesus was anointed by women. [35] For the present purpose it is not necessary to discuss whether or not these are two different occasions; [36] the important point is that Jesus received such worship and affection from women. In the first instance the woman was probably a prostitute, and Jesus' receiving of her act of reverence laid His own character open to question. In the other instance Mary's costly ointment paid highest tribute to the Master, for "this was the kind of demonstration reserved for princes or persons of great distinction." [37] It is a woman who leads the way in saying in effect "that no tribute is rich enough to pay to Him," [38] and this kind of worship He not only receives but defends before all.

If anything is to be made of the words of Jesus that in the resurrection men and women neither marry nor are given in marriage but are like the angels, it would simply be that they show His approval of the purpose of earthly marriage as the perpetuation of the race. [39]

Certain conclusions, some important and some not so important, are evident from these passages. Jesus Christ opened the privileges of religious faith equally to men and to women. He gave His message publicly and privately to women as well as to men. The frequent and prominent mention of women in the gospels is in itself noteworthy by contrast with their status in Judaism. Christ gladly received certain kinds of service from women, including their public testimony. There can be no doubt that as regards *spiritual privilege* Jesus considered the two sexes equal.

However, as regards *spiritual activity,* there was a difference between that of men and women. What is not said about women is as important as what is said. [40] It is significant that Jesus chose and sent out seventy men. [41] It is significant that there was no woman chosen to be among the twelve disciples. It is significant that the Lord's Supper was instituted in the presence of men only. The apostolic commissions of John 20:19–23 and Matthew 28:16–20 were given to men only (though it is true that the Holy Spirit fell upon women as well as men at Pentecost). But it is evident that all these significant facts put together are proof that the activities assigned to women were different from those which our Lord assigned to men. Furthermore, in spite of Harnack's attributing the Epistle to the Hebrews to the pen of Priscilla [42] and Bacon's conjecture that the Revelation was written by one of the four prophesying daughters of Philip the evangelist,[43] it is generally held that no woman was granted the privilege of being the author of any book in the New Testament canon. Surely, then, one must recognize that Jesus Himself differentiated between men and women in their spheres of activity.

In the light of this evidence, the word *revolution* does not seem too strong a word to use of the appreciation of women which Jesus introduced. Though there were definite limitations—things which He did not appreciate, if it may be put that way—His free and merciful attitude toward women introduced a revolutionary appraisal of them. Their spiritual privilege was equal with that of men; definite differences, however, existed in their spiritual activity. And to explain woman's sphere of activity in the gospels is the task of the following chapter.

QUESTIONS

1. How can one tell from the Lord's parables and teachings that there must have been women in His audiences?

2. What was so unusual and significant about the Lord's conversation with the Samaritan woman (John 4)?

3. How does the Lord show clear distinctions between men and women in choosing disciples, choosing writers of the New Testament, and so on?

NOTES

[1] Joseph Barber Lightfoot, *Sermons Preached on Special Occasions* (London, Macmillan, 1891), p. 224.

[2] Donaldson, *Woman* . . . , p. 148.

[3] Allworthy, *Women in the Apostolic Church* (Cambridge: W. Heffer & Sons, 1917), p. 4.

[4] Galatians 3:28.

[5] Matthew 12:50; Mark 3:35; Luke 8:21.

[6] C. G. Montefiore, *Rabbinic Literature and Gospel Teachings* (London, Macmillan, 1930), p. 249.

[7] Luke 12:53.

[8] Allworthy, *loc. cit.*

[9] Matthew 9:20–22; Mark 5:25–34; Luke 8:43–48.

[10] Matthew 15:21–28; Mark 7:25–30.

[11] ". . . the word *kunaria* is in the oriental world, even to-day, an insult." Joachim Jeremias, "The Gentile World in the Thought of Jesus," Bulletin III, *Studiorum Novi Testamenti Societas*, 1952, p. 19.

[12] Matthew 14:21.

[13] Luke 13:18–21.

[14] Matthew 13:2.

[15] Alfred Plummer, *A Critical and Exegetical Commentary on the Gospel According to S. Luke* (Edinburgh, T. & T. Clark, 1901), p. 370.

[16] *Loc. cit.*

[17] Luke 11:5–8; 18:1–5.

[18] Matthew 6:28.

[19] Matthew 24:40–41.

[20] Allworthy, *op. cit.*, p. 5.

[21] John 4:1–42.

[22] *Aboth*, i, 5.

[23] Montefiore, *op. cit.*, p. 47.

[24] *Loc. cit.*

[25] Alfred Edersheim, *The Life and Times of Jesus the Messiah* (Grand Rapids, Eerdmans, 1943), I, 418.

[26] Luke 10:38–42.

[27] Edersheim, *op. cit.*, II, 147.

[28] John 11:1–44.

[29] William Manson, *The Incarnate Glory* (London, James Clarke & Co., 1923), p. 172.

[30] It is omitted by ℵ, A, B, C, L, N, W, Y.

[31] Mark 12:41–44; Luke 21:1–4.

[32] Luke 13:10–17.

[33] Edersheim, *op. cit.*, I, 628.

[34] Luke 8:47.

[35] Luke 7:36–50; John 12:1–11.

[36] Cf. the discussion in Plummer, *op. cit.*, p. 214.

[37] Marcus Dods, *The Gospel of St. John* (London, Hodder & Stoughton, 1908), II, 6. Cf. Psalm 23:5.

[38] *Loc. cit.*

[39] Matthew 22:30; Mark 12:25; Luke 20:35–36. Cf. Henry Latham, *A Service of Angels* (Cambridge, Deighton Bell, 1896), p. 53.

[40] Allworthy, who has been cited several times in this chapter, fails to mention these significant silences in the record. One cannot help feeling that his treatment of Jesus' attitude toward women is unbalanced.

[41] Luke 10:1 ff.

[42] A. Harnack, "Probabilia über die Adresse und den Verfasser des Hebräerbriefs," *Zeitschrift für die neutestamentliche Wissenschaft*, 1900, I, 16–41.

[43] Benjamin W. Bacon, "The Authoress of Revelation—A Conjecture," *Harvard Theological Review*, Vol. xxiii, No. 33, pp. 235–250.

Chapter IV

WOMEN AS MINISTERS TO JESUS

Absolutely unique in the gospels is the place accorded to women as ministers to the person of the Lord Jesus Christ. "Our Lord's relations with the women who attended Him are distinct from His relations with the men disciples in one very remarkable particular. He ministered to men; but the women ministered to Him. In their case Jesus consented to receive gifts and service."[1] The occurrences of *diakoneō*, to serve, and its cognates in the four gospels show at once that whenever ministry is spoken of as being rendered directly to Jesus, it is the ministry of either angels or of women. After the temptation angels "came and ministered unto him."[2] All of the other instances speak of the ministry of women. After her healing, Peter's mother-in-law ministered to the Lord and the others in the house.[3] Mention is made of a band of women who "ministered unto him of their substance,"[4] and on two occasions it is recorded that Martha served Jesus.[5]

Although *diakoneō* may be used in an official sense of serving as deacons or in a general sense of attending to anything, especially the supplying of necessities of life,[6] it is used in this latter and general sense of the women who ministered to Jesus in the gospels. Martha waited on the table, the band of women provided money, and Peter's mother-in-law evidently provided food for that occasion. Here, then, is the key to understanding the particular sphere of service of women in the gospels, and theirs was a different honor from that of the other followers of the Master.

Jewish scribes were supposed to support themselves financially by practicing some trade, for every Jewish father's obligations to

34

his son were to "circumcise him, redeem him, teach him Torah, teach him a trade, and get him a wife—some say also, teach him to swim."[7] In the time of Christ, however, many scribes had evidently given up making a livelihood by means of a trade and were accepting the support of well-to-do women. Josephus mentions an instance of the abuse of this practice,[8] and our Lord Himself also spoke out against its abuse.[9] However, that it might be done without impropriety is evident from the fact that no surprise is shown or criticism leveled at Jesus' receiving money from wealthy women. The first mention of this band of ministering women is found in Luke 8:2-3:

And certain women, which had been healed of evil spirits and infirmities, Mary called Magdalene, out of whom went seven devils, and Joanna the wife of Chuza Herod's steward, and Susanna, and many others, which ministered unto him of their substance.

Actually, this is the only passage in the gospels which tells how Jesus and His disciples lived when they were not being entertained by hospitable persons. As Plummer observes: "The common purse (Jn. xiii. 29; comp. xii. 6) was kept supplied by the generosity of pious women. This form of piety was not rare."[10]

Five of this ministering band who followed Jesus throughout His ministry are mentioned by name (Mary Magdalene, Joanna, Susanna, Mary, Salome), but each of the synoptic writers records that there were many others.[11] One writer believes that Joanna and Salome were widows, because "we cannot for a moment suppose that our Lord would have approved of married women, with home duties, neglecting them for ministry to Himself."[12] While this would be a convenient conclusion, it could hardly be substantiated in these two cases, to say nothing of the "many others." In every list of these women in the synoptics the name of Mary Magdalene stands first.[13] Her circumstances were probably less humble than other disciples of Christ, and consequently her part in maintaining the common purse was likely larger than that of the others. In the apocryphal Gospel of Peter she is called "a disciple of the Lord."[14]

Godet thinks that Joanna was the wife of Chuza who "was probably entrusted with some office in the household of Herod Antipas. Might he not be that *basilikos, court lord,* whose son Jesus healed (John iv.), and who had believed *with all his house?*" [15] Susanna, Mary the mother of James the less and wife of Clopas, and Salome are the only other women mentioned by name.[16] These plus the "many others" ministered to Jesus of their substance and followed Him from place to place.

However, it is in the accounts of the crucifixion and the resurrection that women assume a prominent place. Some of this band of ministering women followed Christ to Jerusalem to the last Passover and were found at the scene of the crucifixion.[17] At some point during the hours of crucifixion they evidently moved within talking distance of the cross,[18] and they followed the body of their Lord to the place of His burial in order to minister to Him by preparing the spices and ointments.[19] But since it was the Sabbath day they rested, and coming the next day with those spices they found the tomb empty.

According to the Biblical record, it seems clear that women were the first to receive the news of our Lord's resurrection.[20] Not only that, but they were the first to carry the news of that resurrection, [21] and although their word was not believed immediately by the disciples, the Lord's rebuke of the disciples shows that He expected them to believe.[22] However, this evidence must be weighed against the fact that St. Paul does not include a single woman's name in the list of witnesses he cites when writing to the Corinthians.[23] Three questions thus arise: (1) Why did God choose women to be the first recipients of the news of the resurrection? (2) Why does Paul omit entirely any mention of women in his list of witnesses? (3) What conclusions may be drawn from all of this concerning the status of women?

A variety of answers to the first question has been suggested. Allworthy makes this sweeping statement: "This privilege [of knowing of the resurrection first] alone must have secured, not for the women disciples only but for their sex, a position of honour in the Church of the first days." [24] This can hardly be true, since it ignores the important fact that these women were told, on the occasion of the resurrection at least, to go tell the male disciples, not the whole world. Also, if the assertion be true, why was not a woman nominated to fill Judas' place among the twelve disciples? The correct answer to the question of why God chose women to receive the news first has often been missed because it is so obvious. Women were honored with the news of the resurrection first simply because they were being faithful to womanly duties. After all, they were present at the tomb that first Easter morning because they were bringing spices for the body, something they had been prevented from doing earlier because of the Sabbath. This was a woman's work—not a man's—and they were ministering in caring for physical needs in the time of death as they had so often done during the time of Jesus' life. God so honored them because of their faithful performance of the responsibilities of their sex.

The well-known answer to the second question, Why did St. Paul omit the mention of the women's testimony in I Corinthians 15? is that since the witness of women could not be official, it could not be used in that context. In other words, "Outside Christian circles, the evidence of women would have been dismissed of little value. Had it been adduced, it would have been ridiculed as the fantasies of excitable females." [25] This view does not go unchallenged. Knowling says:

But let us bear in mind the official character of the Apostle's selection, and we shall see at once that he appeals to those by name who would claim special credit in the Church, and that it would be nothing to the point to lay stress upon the testimony of women whose names, however valued elsewhere, would carry little or no weight in Corinth. [26]

Before accepting this answer, however, one should ask, What was Paul's purpose in that chapter? It was to prove that Jesus "was seen." [27] Does this require quality or quantity of witnesses? Both, of course. Otherwise, of what point is his mention of the five hundred brethren of whom a majority were alive at that time? [28] It is unlikely that any of that group lived in Corinth, and certainly the mention of them would mean very little except as they added to the total number of living witnesses of the resurrection. If quantity is partly Paul's point, then why did he not also add "and a number of women?" There must have been some reason for the omission of a phrase like that, and because of it we are driven back to the conclusion that it was simply that the witness of women would lack official status. That original answer is strengthened by the fact that in the second century the objection that the women's story was the "fantasies of excitable females" was raised by Celsus.[29] The well-known answer, then, seems also to be the most satisfactory one. It does not nullify the validity of the testimony of women nor diminish the honor accorded them as first witnesses of the empty tomb; it simply, once again, shows the limitation of the sphere of their work.

The third question, Of what significance is all this? has practically been answered, and well summarizes this chapter. In the life of our Lord women had a very special place as ministers to Him in a sense in which no man was His minister. This ministry consisted in caring for His physical wants by hospitality, by giving of money, and preparing spices for His dead body. In response to this, Jesus allowed the women to follow Him, He taught them, and He honored them with the first announcement of His resurrection. But, equally important, He limited their activity by not choosing one of them for official work. Thus we may say that, while Jesus granted great freedom to women and placed importance on their ministrations, He limited the sphere of their activity by glorifying the domestic responsibilities with which they ministered to Him.

QUESTIONS

1. How is the word that means "to serve" used in the Gospels?
2. Did women help with the financial support of the band of disciples?
3. Why were women the first to receive the news of the resurrection?

NOTES

[1] Walter F. Adeney, *Women of the New Testament* (London, James Nisbet & Co., 1901), p. 100.

[2] Matthew 4:11; Mark 1:13.

[3] Matthew 8:15; Mark 1:31; Luke 4:39.

[4] Luke 8:3; cf. Matthew 27:55 and Mark 15:41.

[5] Luke 10:40; John 12:2.

[6] Walter Bauer, *Griechisch-Deutsches Wörterbuch* (Berlin, A. Topelmann, 1952), p. 333.

[7] Moore, *Judaism*, II, 127.

[8] "For there was a certain sect of men that were Jews, who valued themselves highly upon the exact skill they had in the law of their fathers, and made men believe they were highly favored by God, by whom this set of women were inveigled" (*Antiquities*, XVII, II, 4).

[9] Mark 12:40; Luke 20:47.

[10] Plummer, *A Commentary . . . on S. Luke*, p. 215.

[11] Matthew 27:55; Mark 15:41; Luke 8:3.

[12] John Wordsworth, *The Ministry of Grace* (London, Longmans, Green & Co., 1901), p. 259.

[13] But cf. John 19:25.

[14] XII:50. The word used is *mathētria*, which is found in the N.T. only at Acts 9:36.

[15] F. Godet, *A Commentary on the Gospel of St. Luke* (Edinburgh, T. & T. Clark, 1890), I, 365.

[16] Luke 8:3; Matthew 27:56; Mark 15:40; Luke 24:10; John 19:25.

[17] Matthew 27:55; Mark 15:40; Luke 23:49.

[18] John 19:25.

[19] Luke 23:55–56.

[20] Matthew 28:1; Mark 16:1; Luke 24:1; John 20:1.

[21] Matthew 28:7; Mark 16:7; Luke 24:9; John 20:17.

[22] Mark 16:11, 14.

[23] I Corinthians 15:5–7.

[24] Allworthy, *Women in the Apostolic Church*, p. 13.

[25] F. F. Bruce, *The Dawn of Christianity* (London, Paternoster Press, 1950), p. 68.

[26] R. J. Knowling, *The Testimony of St. Paul to Christ* (London, Hodder & Stoughton, 1905), pp. 301–302.

[27] I Corinthians 15:5.

[28] I Corinthians 15:6.

[29] Origen, *Against Celsus*, II, 58.

Chapter V

JESUS' TEACHING ON DIVORCE

Some of the most clear and definite revelations of the mind of Christ concerning the status of women in the church are found in His teaching on divorce. The Lord's contribution in this matter is of such significance and importance that Montefiore can say of it without exaggeration: "If he had done no more than this, he might justly be regarded as one of the great teachers of the world." [1] His teaching was a radically new departure and proposed a considerably higher standard than that of His day; yet, a statement like that necessitates solving the many difficulties and problems of determining the precise mind of the Lord on this subject. Consequently, our first task is to try to determine what His exact teaching on this subject was.

THE HISTORICAL SITUATION

Jewish law allowed for divorce on almost any ground once proceedings had been initiated, for "there was no marriage among the Jewish people which could not have been dissolved immediately by the man in fully legal form by handing out a bill of divorce." [2] The Biblical basis for this was Deuteronomy 24:1—especially the words *'erwath dabhar*. In the time of Christ it was not a question of whether or not a man had the right of divorce, for that was guaranteed by law; but on what grounds he might set the law in motion was the question which divided the Rabbis. Divorces were granted because a woman merely broke a single part of the Mosaic law, or when the behavior of a woman was such as to put her husband in a bad light, or because of barrenness, or if illness or the occupation

of the husband was such as to make continued living with him unthinkable.[3]

Principally, however, there were two schools of thought, at the
time of Christ, on the interpretation of Deuteronomy 24:1. The followers of Shammai were strict and rigorous interpreters of the law,
for they read *'erwath dabhar* as "uncleanness of behavior," and
emphasized "uncleanness." Consequently they held that a man
could not divorce his wife unless he found her guilty of sexual
immorality. On the other hand, the school of Hillel was more lax
in its interpretation, disjoining the words *'erwath dabhar* and reading them "uncleanness, or anything else." Being more lenient, this
interpretation enjoyed greater popularity and was usually followed.[4]
Nevertheless, opposition between the two schools of thought remained strong. It is easy to understand then why the Pharisees,
when they came tempting the Lord about this matter, asked Him if
it were legal for a man to put away his wife "for every cause." [5]
They hoped to force the Lord to take a view which would support
a lower moral standard or one that would make Him less popular
with the people.[6]

This was the historical situation into which our Lord's teaching
was cast. The right of divorce was unquestioned and was primarily
the man's. It is very important to remember that none of the
Rabbis prohibited divorce, for even among the strict school of
Shammai it was not a question of the right of divorce but of the
ground of divorce. No wonder the teaching of Christ was startling.

THE TEACHING OF JESUS

Jesus' teaching on divorce is found in Matthew 5:31–32, Matthew
19:3–9, Mark 10:2–12, and Luke 16:18. Although there are many
problems and questions connected with these passages, certain
things are clear. First of all, it is clear that Jesus' teaching was
startling to His hearers, for the disciples said, "If the case of the
man be so with his wife, it is not good to marry." [7] Their reaction
evidently shows that they understood that: "The standard here set
up was so high, the law so severe in its obligations, that, fearing
when there should be no possibility of putting a complete end to

the union, its trials and temptations might prove unbearable, they suggested that, under the circumstances, the wisest course would be to abjure marriage altogether." [8] In reply our Lord does not say that celibacy is to be preferred, but the very fact that the disciples even suggested it shows that they understood Jesus' teaching to be something startlingly different from what they knew in Judaism, and "in the answer which Christ gave, there is not the slightest hint that they had exaggerated the force of His teaching. . . ." [9]

Not only was this doctrine startling, but it was more rigid than the accepted Jewish standard of the day. In the first place, the one-sidedness of the Jewish law respecting adultery is corrected. The point is well explained in the following words:

. . . the essential point is that in Jewish Law adultery is *always* intercourse between a married woman and a man other than her husband. . . . Hence while a woman can commit adultery against her husband, a man cannot commit adultery against his wife. He can only commit adultery against another married man. . . . The principle that a man cannot commit adultery against his own wife is flatly contradicted in Mk. 10, where the words "against her" can only refer to the first wife. [10]

In the second place, Jesus, instead of taking sides with either the school of Shammai or that of Hillel, leads His hearers back to the original institution of marriage. He shows that originally the bond was intended to be indissoluble and that divorce under the Mosaic law was only by permission and because of the hardness of their hearts. In other words, the Lord removes divorce, and all that is involved in relation to the status of women, from under Jewish legal jurisdiction and elevates marriage and women to the ideal state described at the institution of marriage in Genesis before the fall of man and the entrance of sin. "Jesus . . . undertook to say what, on ideal principles, the law ought to be, Moses to the contrary notwithstanding." [11]

In the third place, Jesus had a word to say about divorce in relation to Roman law. In the time of Herod, Roman law allowed women to divorce their husbands, and under this law divorces were given by the women of Herod's family. This "seems to have attracted the attention of Jesus, and he strongly condemned it, saying, 'if a woman shall put away her husband and be married to another she committeth adultery' . . ." [12] Therefore, the teaching of Jesus was of a higher standard than both the religious and political law of His time.

THE PROBLEM IN MATTHEW'S GOSPEL

It must be clear from what has been said that this writer believes that Jesus did not allow for divorce at all. However, this has not been proved, for we have not dealt with the "excepting clause" in Matthew's gospel. [13] If Jesus did not disallow divorce entirely He allowed it in the single instance of fornication, and if He did then He did not rise in His standards much above the school of Shammai. There are multitudinous explanations of the "excepting clause," but fortunately these may be sifted into three categories.

Explanation based on the authority of the church. As one might expect, the Roman Catholic Church bases its explanation on the dogma of the Church. That Church, of course, admits no exception that sanctions divorce, but she is faced with the problem of making all the texts consistent. One of their theologians says that "that explanation is at once found if we consider that the words 'put away' in St. Matthew refer to separation only and not to dissolution." [14] This explanation that *apoluō* means separation from bed and board was one of the decrees of the Council of Trent. Of course, there is no necessity for substantiating grammatically such a meaning for *apoluō*, for the real reason for such an explanation is revealed in another statement by the same man: "What we have given seems the simplest explanation of the difficulty . . . and the matter affords a good instance of the impossibility of arriving at any assured interpretation of Scripture, except in the light of the traditional teaching of the Catholic Church." [15] One would not even submit this view as a worthy explanation of the difficulty.

Explanation based on the evidence of source criticism. The usual Protestant interpretation of the texts may be stated thus:

. . . that the exceptive clause in the first Gospel is an interpolation, which really alters the sense of our Lord's original utterance about marriage, and that His real teaching is that given in St. Mark's and St. Luke's Gospels. . . .[16]

If one believes that the compiler of Matthew used Mark and Q as his sources, then there is little question that the exception in Matthew 19 (which is parallel to Mark 10) is an interpolation. Very likely that also is the case in Matthew 5, although this would be more difficult to prove because the original form of the saying drawn from Q in this case is considered uncertain. Nevertheless, those who favor this conclusion that Mark's record prohibiting divorce entirely represents the true mind of Christ cite other considerations.

The first is suggested by Salmon:

. . . it seems to me that St Mark's version, which appears to disallow divorce without any exception, is more likely to represent the common source than St Matthew's, which excepts the case of the adulterous wife. For it is much easier to account for St Matthew's insertion of the words than for St Mark's omission of them, if they had been in the original.[17]

The second is an argument from context, for if the Lord taught an absolute standard as Mark indicates, then according to the context of Matthew 5 "teaching such as this is entirely in harmony with the teaching about murder (21–24) and about adultery (27, 28), and is above the level of the best Jewish teaching." [18]

Finally, W. C. Allen suggests a third reason for concluding that the excepting clause is a gloss. He suggests that "the interpolated clause confuses the issues. If a man divorced his wife for *porneia,* he would not then cause her to commit adultery, because she would already be guilty of this crime." [19]

R. H. Charles disagrees with such a line of reasoning and at-

tempts to show from the documentary evidence that Mark is un-
reliable and that the excepting clause should be retained as representing the mind of Jesus. He says:

Thus it is shown not only that the narrative in Mark x. 2–12 is
untrustworthy, but also that the First Evangelist (Matt. xix. 3–9)
deliberately rejected the Marcan record as unhistorical and replaced
it by a record of events drawn from Q . . .

. . . it follows that the original narrative in Q, from which Matt.
xix. 3–9 and Luke xvi. 18 are independently derived, was not designed to prove the indissolubility of marriage, but to condemn
divorce when resorted to on inadequate grounds. . . .[20]

Thus Charles contends that the uncertain contents of Q contained
the words of exception and are to be accepted in preference to the
Marcan record. Is it not a very weak argument which rejects a
source we do have as "untrustworthy" on the basis of the supposed
contents of one we do not have? Actually, Charles' real basis for
his conclusion is not source criticism but historical considerations,
for he declares that Mark is to be considered unhistorical for omit-
ting the excepting clause since such an answer "would have been
incomprehensible to a Jew in the time of our Lord."[21] But that is
just the point. The Pharisees did not come to Jesus to ask for information or clarification but to try to draw from Him something
with which they could accuse Him, and our Lord's answer was new,
startling, and in a real sense incomprehensible. If He had admitted
an exception He would have aligned Himself with the school of
Shammai and could have been accused of undue strictness.

The explanation on the basis of source criticism is that Jesus forbade divorce and that the exception clause in Matthew is an added
interpolation, "representing no doubt two influences, viz. Jewish
custom and tradition and the exigencies of ethical necessity in the
early Christian Church."[22]

Explanation based on the authority of inspiration. For those who
believe in the verbal, plenary inspiration of the Scriptures, neither

of the above explanations is satisfactory. The explanation based on the authority of the Roman Church could not be accepted, and since the excepting clause must be accounted a genuine part of the text, it cannot be called a gloss without damaging the doctrine of verbal inspiration; thus another explanation must be found. There are some in this group who solve the difficulty and come to the conclusion (for the Scripture cannot contradict itself and a gloss is unthinkable) that fornication is a legitimate reason for divorce. Such a conclusion, of course, means that the Lord's teaching was not startling and did not rise above standards held by certain ones in His own day. John Murray's careful work on divorce furnishes an example of this viewpoint:

We are compelled to take the position that if the exceptive clause belongs to Matthew's Gospel, then it truly represents our Lord's teaching. It would be incompatible with the inspiration of Scripture to reject Matthew in favour of Mark and Luke, as it would also be to reject Mark and Luke in favour of Matthew. . . . In such a case the accounts in Matthew would simply affirm that there is one exception to the rule that whoever puts away his wife causes her to commit adultery, namely, antecedent adultery on the part of the wife herself.[23]

However, it has always seemed to this writer that such an answer to the problem did not give full consideration to the question, Why did Mark and Luke not mention the exception of fornication? The average conservative seems so happy to find one legitimate cause for divorce that he does not realize that his conclusion actually places the accounts in Mark and Luke in the category of contradictions. The average dispensationalist goes a step further in contradiction by accepting as a standard for the church age something revealed in Matthew's gospel and particularly in the Sermon on the Mount. This is done in spite of the clear Pauline dictum (which he, Paul, evidently believed reflected the teaching of Christ): "Let not the husband put away his wife."[24] Thus it has appeared to this writer that there must be some other solution which better explains all the facts in the texts. The explanation, which does not violate the doctrine of verbal, plenary inspiration and yet which is aware of the textual evidence and which leads to the conclusion that Jesus forbade divorce altogether, is suggested by W. K. Lowther Clarke, who himself would not hold this view of inspiration. Specifically the solution is that *porneia* denotes marital relations within the forbidden degrees of Leviticus 18. In outlining his view Clarke says:

Porneia cannot have meant infidelity within the realm of marriage, for in Matt. xv. 19 it is distinguished from *moicheia*. For St. Matthew infidelity between betrothal and marriage would have been adultery (*moicheia*), see 1. 19. . . .

Two passages throw light on the word. In 1 Cor. v. 1 St. Paul denounces a heinous form of *porneia,* a man's marrying his father's widow. . . .

The Apostolic Decree of Acts xv. 29 promulgated a compromise by which Gentiles and Jews could share a common social life, and with it the Eucharist: the Gentiles were to abstain from meat sold at the butcher's which had played its part at a sacrifice, from meat at the killing of which the blood had not been properly drained, from "black-puddings" and other repellent ways of using the blood, and from "fornication" (*porneia*). . . . Since the first three articles of the compromise are concerned with practices innocent enough to the Gentiles, the fourth must be of a similar nature. The passage in 1 Corinthians gives us the clue. *Porneia* here means *marriage within the prohibited Levitical degrees.* . . . But for a decade or two, especially in places like Antioch, where Jew and Gentile met and where the agitation which led to the decree arose, *marriage within the prohibited degrees* was a live issue, and *porneia* was the word by which it was known.

Turning to St. Matthew, the problem we have to account for is the obscuring of the plain rule of St. Mark by an exception which seems inconsistent with the teaching of our Lord even in St. Matthew. If the foregoing argument holds, the reference is to the local Syrian problem. One exception is allowed to the universal rule:

when a man who has married within the prohibited degrees puts away his wife the word adultery is out of place. Rather the marriage is null. . . .

If this solution is correct, the famous excepting clause, so far from being a flaw in the Church's case, strengthens it. There is no divorce, but causes of nullity may be recognized.[25]

This is the solution which personally appeals to the writer as being the most consistent with the texts and his own doctrine of inspiration. However, it should be noted carefully that the solution offered by the Roman dogma, the solution offered in source criticism by the more liberal scholar, and this solution offered by one who believes in verbal inspiration, all agree in the conclusion important to this book; that is, that our Lord's teaching on divorce did not allow for it under any circumstances but rather placed marriage on that ideal plane described in Genesis. What this did to elevate the status of women I doubt that many of us living in this century can grasp.[26]

CONCLUSIONS

A word of summary is in order. The idea was proposed in this chapter that Jesus announced a new and superior doctrine concerning marriage and divorce which brought a corresponding elevation of the status of women in His day. To substantiate this, it was shown that He went further in His teaching than the strictest Jews of the day by disallowing divorce altogether. The "excepting clause" of Matthew is not an exception, and all explanations led to the conclusion that divorce was disallowed. Although our Lord did not blame Moses for allowing a bill of divorce, He replaced the Jewish law with God's ideal state.

What does all of this show about the status of women? Chiefly it emphasizes the exalted and inviolable position of women as partners with their husbands, for the Lord Jesus said that the starting place for a proper understanding of the status of women is in Genesis. The perfect and permanent union until death of man and woman who become one flesh [27] and who are therefore equal and yet different is the chief emphasis of Christ's teaching concerning divorce, and this was far superior to any other teaching of His day. All of this is a prelude to the elaboration of this same emphasis in the epistles of the New Testament.

QUESTIONS

1. On what grounds did the Jews allow divorce?
2. How do we know that Jesus' teaching on divorce was startling to the disciples?
3. What is the "excepting clause" in Matthew's gospel?
4. How do the Roman Catholics interpret it?
5. How do liberals interpret it?
6. In what two ways do conservatives explain it? Which seems the better?
7. How did the Lord's teaching on divorce affect the status of women?

NOTES

[1] Montefiore, *Rabbinic Literature,* p. 47.
[2] Hermann L. Strack and Paul Billerbeck, *Kommentar zum Neuen Testament* (München, Oskar Beck, 1922), I, 319–320.
[3] Cf. Strack and Billerbeck, *op. cit.,* I, 312–320, and David Werner Amram, *The Jewish Law of Divorce* (London, D. Nutt, 1897), pp. 41–53, 63–77.
[4] *Gittin,* ix. 10.
[5] Matthew 19:3.
[6] The teaching of the Zadokites in Damascus in the first century B.C., which included monogamy and the forbidding of divorce, had little or no influence on the main stream of Jewish life. Cf. R. H. Charles, editor, *The Apocrypha and Pseudepigrapha of the Old Testament* (Oxford, Clarendon Press, 1913), II, 810.
[7] Matthew 19:10.
[8] Herbert Mortimer Lucklock, *The History of Marriage* (London, Longmans, Green & Co., 1894), p. 70.
[9] *Loc. cit.*
[10] H. D. A. Major, T. W. Manson, C. J. Wright, *The Mission and Message of Jesus* (New York, E. P. Dutton & Co., 1937), p. 428.
[11] Moore, *Judaism,* II, 125.
[12] Amram, *op. cit.,* pp. 61–62.
[13] Matthew 5:32; 19:9.
[14] Sylvester Joseph Hunter, *Outline of Dogmatic Theology* (London, Longmans, Green & Co., 1900), III, 416.
[15] *Loc. cit.*
[16] Charles Gore, *The Question of Divorce* (London, John Murray, 1911), p. 23.
[17] George Salmon, *The Human Element in the Gospels* (London, John Murray, 1908), pp. 130–131.
[18] Alfred Plummer, *An Exegetical Commentary on the Gospel According to S. Matthew* (London, E. Stock, 1909), p. 81.

[19] *A Critical and Exegetical Commentary on the Gospel According to S. Matthew* (Edinburgh, T. & T. Clark, 1907), p. 51.

[20] R. H. Charles, *Divorce and the Roman Dogma of Nullity* (Edinburgh, T. & T. Clark, 1927), pp. v–vii.

[21] *Ibid.*, p. 17.

[22] Allen, *op. cit.*, p. 52. This is further supported by Bacon's contention that "Mt is a 'converted rabbi.' His ideal, his methods . . . all show the characteristics of the trained teacher of the Synagogue." Cf. Benjamin W. Bacon, *Studies in Matthew* (New York, Henry Holt & Co., 1930), p. 132.

[23] John Murray, *Divorce* (Philadelphia, Committee on Christian Education, Orthodox Presbyterian Church, 1953), pp. 47–48. For a less thorough approach which arrives at the same conclusion cf. F. C. Jennings, *Does Death Alone Break the Marriage Relation?* (New York, Loizeaux Bros., 1931), p. 28.

[24] I Corinthians 7:11.

[25] W. K. Lowther Clarke, *New Testament Problems* (New York, Macmillan, 1929), pp. 59–60.

[26] One must never let practical problems or implications determine a doctrine. Everything in the New Testament points to the disallowance of divorce, including the important evidence of Paul's interpretation of Christ's teaching in I Corinthians 7:11. Like so many Christian standards in the New Testament, marriage is placed on this ideal plane. If some difficulty causes a marriage to fall short of this, then there may be in some instances no other solution which the spiritually minded minister can allow but divorce. But the standard remains ideal, not an ideal with one exception.

[27] Genesis 2:24.

PART II

The Place of Women
in the Life of the Church
During the Apostolic Age

Chapter VI

WOMEN AND THE FOUNDING OF THE CHURCH

The Apostolic Age is the period from Pentecost to the end of the first century, or the period covered by the New Testament except for the gospels. During this period women had an important part in the founding of the church—a phase of their activity which is often overlooked. I suppose that in their thinking about this subject many Christians never get past certain passages in Paul which deal with the status of women, and consequently they miss seeing the large place women occupied in the early missionary activity of the church. Harnack rightly says that "no one who reads the New Testament . . . can fail to notice that in the apostolic and subapostolic age women played an important role in the propaganda of Christianity and throughout the Christian communities." [1] And yet some do fail to notice this; hence the reason for this chapter.

Immediately after Christ's ascension women gathered with the apostles and disciples in the upper room in Jerusalem. They were not there to cook for the men but to pray with them, and there is certainly no reason to believe that they were not included in the group who prayed for Judas' successor. Nothing could be more unlikely than that Mary and the other women were asked to withdraw at that point in the proceedings. The group probably included those women mentioned earlier who ministered to Jesus, and there is no reason to exclude them from the number of 120 disciples. [2]

In the very first weeks of the history of the church there were not many women converts, [3] but that condition did not last long. After the death of Ananias and Sapphira "believers were the more added to the Lord, multitudes both of men and women," [4] and by the time of the first scattering women were mentioned as particular objects of the persecution.[5] All of this gives some indication of their increasing number. One of these early Jerusalem converts, Mary the mother of John Mark, donated her house as a meeting place for part of the church in that city. Indeed, it must have been an important meeting place, because Peter made his way there almost automatically after his release from prison.[6] Some authorities believe that the upper room was in her house.[7]

When the gospel reached Samaria, again the record mentions the women who believed it and who were baptized along with the men. Why is it not true, too, that they were among those upon whom the apostles laid hands and who received the gift of the Holy Spirit?[8] When the Christian message went into Europe, women again were prominent in the record. The first European convert was a woman named Lydia, "a seller of purple of the city of Thyatira."[9] Because she is mentioned as head of her household[10] she was probably a widow, and evidently she was a wealthy one. Shortly after her conversion another woman, a demon-possessed slave, also believed the message—an illustration of how the gospel is able to reach all classes.[11] It is not at all unlikely that among the women who gathered with Lydia at the *Proseuchē* and who were converted in the early days of the mission in Philippi were Euodia and Syntyche.[12] Lightfoot suggests that at the time of the writing of the Philippian letter they were deaconesses in that church,[13] while Harnack[14] and Vincent[15] both suggest that two congregations met in their respective houses. Whatever was their position in the Philippian church, they held a place of honor and usefulness— perhaps even in evangelistic work—since they are said to have wrestled together with Paul in the gospel.[16]

Both in Thessalonica and Berea there were honorable women among those who believed.[17] "Honorable women" likely means wives of leading citizens of the community[18] who were probably reached with the gospel simply because the social position of women was higher and more free in Macedonia than in most parts of the civilized world.[19] In Athens one woman, Damaris, is mentioned among the few converts whom Paul had in that city.[20] She was probably one of the *hetairai* since no Greek woman of respectable position would have been present in St. Paul's audience on Mars' hill.[21]

It is, however, in the story of the work at Corinth that one of the most interesting women of the period is introduced. Priscilla is mentioned along with her husband six times in the New Testament, and in four of these instances her name stands first.[22] Although there can be little doubt that she was a woman of culture and education,[23] her precedence is due primarily to "her greater fervency of spirit or ability of character."[24] Her ability to instruct the cultured Greek Apollos is probably only one of the many ways in which she served the church. One would like very much to know exactly in what ways she ministered or was active in the church in her house,[25] for she could hardly be excluded from the ranks of a teacher, though whether she exercised a public teaching ministry is an unanswerable question.

One of the most startling evidences of the prominence of women is found in the last chapter of the Epistle to the Romans where eight women are named among the twenty-six persons specifically mentioned in that chapter. The question is, however, What kind of work did they do? Phoebe's case, which will be discussed in full in another chapter, furnishes part of the answer to that question. Priscilla in verse 3 is called a helper, *sunergos*, of Paul. Probably the term is to be understood as signifying the help she gave the church by furnishing a meeting place for the local group and whatever private instruction she gave as in the case of Apollos. Admittedly it would be difficult to prove that the "helping" did not include public teaching and even possibly missionary work. And yet, if this were the case one is surprised not to find mention of it elsewhere in the New Testament.

Mary, mentioned in verse six, evidently performed a personal ministry for Paul like that of the women who ministered to Christ during His life. The problem of verse 7 is determining the correct gender of the name Junia which appears in the accusative form Iounian. It might be from Iounias (masculine) or from Iounia (feminine). Some are afraid to see this as a feminine form because

that might mean that a woman was "of note among the apostles."
However, that phrase "of note among the apostles," *episēmoi en
tois apostolois,* may mean, it is true, "distinguished as apostles" or,
equally accurately, "well-known to the apostles." Thus before one
could say that Junia was a female apostle he would have to prove a
feminine nominative from the ambiguous accusative and establish
that *episēmoi* meant "of note" and not merely "well-known." Though
Junia is undoubtedly a woman, she was not an apostle. One other
woman stands out in this list, and she is the mother of Rufus
mentioned in verse 13. Paul calls her "his mother," which probably
means "that this matron—whoever she may have been—had at
some time shown him motherly kindness, which he had requited
with filial affection." [26]

The import of these passages is well stated by Knowling:

St. Paul has sometimes been accused of a want of due respect
towards women. This last chapter of his Epistle to the Romans is
sufficient in itself to refute such a charge. From the beginning to
the end, the writer chooses with the most apt consideration the
title and the merit which belongs to each member of the household
of God, and recognizes the special work which a woman, and
often only a woman, can do in the church.[27]

Thus in the early propagation of the Christian message women
played an important role. The number of times specific women are
mentioned in the accounts of the founding of various churches is in
itself striking. In many instances a woman's home was the meeting
place for the church.[28] Some, like Priscilla, Apphia,[29] Euodia, and
Syntyche, were doubtless leaders in their respective assemblies.
Mary, Rufus' mother, and others evidently succored the church with
a quieter ministry, and women in large numbers and with full
privileges came into the church from its earliest days. That they
played an important role is beyond question.

But, it must be added, to say that women played a leading role
is another matter. The incarnation was in a man; the apostles were
all men; the chief missionary activity was done by men; the writing

of the New Testament was the work of men; and, in general, the leadership of the churches was entrusted to men. Nevertheless, a prominence and dignity which women did not have either in Judaism or in the heathen world was theirs in the early propagation and expansion of Christianity, the historical record of which would be immeasurably poorer without this prominence, secondary though it was.

QUESTIONS

1. In what ways did Priscilla serve the Church?
2. Name some of the women who evidently opened their homes to the early church for meeting places.
3. Name some of the things which women did *not* do in the early days of the expansion of the church.

NOTES

[1] Adolf Harnack, *The Mission and Expansion of Christianity in the First Three Centuries* (London, Williams & Norgate, 1908), II, 64.

[2] Acts 1:15. Deissmann has clearly shown that *onoma* here means "person" and can include persons of the female sex. Cf. Adolf Deissmann, *Bible Studies* (Edinburgh, T. & T. Clark, 1901), p. 196.

[3] Cf. the use in Acts 4:4 of *anēr*, which signifies only males.

[4] Acts 5:14.

[5] Acts 8:3.

[6] Acts 12:12.

[7] Cf. W. Sanday, *Sacred Sites of the Gospels* (Oxford, Clarendon Press, 1903), p. 83.

[8] Acts 8:12–17.

[9] Acts 16:14.

[10] Acts 16:40.

[11] Acts 16:16, 19.

[12] Philippians 4:2.

[13] J. B. Lightfoot, *Saint Paul's Epistle to the Philippians* (London, Macmillan, 1896), p. 55.

[14] Harnack, *op. cit.*, II, 67.

[15] Marvin R. Vincent, *Philippians* (Edinburgh, T. & T. Clark, 1897), p. 130.

[16] Philippians 4:3.

[17] Acts 17:4, 12.

[18] Cf. Richard Belward Rackham, *The Acts of the Apostles* (London, Methuen, 1901), p. 295.

[19] Cf. Lightfoot, *op. cit.*, pp. 55–56.

[20] Acts 17:34.

[21] Cf. W. M. Ramsay, *The Church in the Roman Empire* (London, Hodder & Stoughton, 1893), p. 160.

[22] Acts 18:2, 26; Romans 16:3; I Corinthians 16:19; II Timothy 4:19.

[23] Acts 18:26.

[24] R. J. Knowling, *The Acts of the Apostles* (London, Hodder & Stoughton, 1900), II, 384.

[25] I Corinthians 16:19.

[26] Alice Gardner, "St. Paul and Women," *The Ministry of Women* (London, SPCK, 1919), p. 43.

[27] R. J. Knowling, *The Testimony of St. Paul to Christ* (London, Hodder & Stoughton, 1905), p. 466.

[28] Cf. also Nymphas, Colossians 4:15, who is probably another example of a woman who furnished her home as a meeting place for the church.

[29] Philemon's wife, who, though probably not any sort of official in that church, was of sufficient importance to merit special mention in the Epistle to Philemon.

Chapter VII

THE DOMESTIC STATUS OF WOMEN

New Testament passages which discuss matters related to marriage, celibacy, divorce, and the home furnish further evidence of the status of women in the early years of the Christian church. Three such passages are especially pertinent: (1) Paul's answer to questions sent him concerning marriage by the Corinthian Church; [1] (2) the relation of husband and wife as set forth in Ephesians; [2] (3) and Peter's discussion of proper demeanor and deportment for women.[3] None of these passages is without difficulties, some of which are relevant to this discussion and some of which are not. Unfortunately, some of the discussion must of necessity be technical; otherwise, the conclusions will be inaccurate. A historian must report the facts; in addition he will also inquire into the causes which helped shape the facts; finally, he will at least pose the question to his readers, What relevance and application do these facts have to the place of women today? This will be the procedure of this chapter.

MARRIAGE, CELIBACY, AND RELATED MATTERS

Chief among the characteristics of Corinth in St. Paul's day was that it was a city of pleasure. Its position on the crossroads of trade routes both north and south as well as east and west made it a very cosmopolitan city and contributed to its immorality. However, this immoral character of Corinth was not only the kind which comes to a cosmopolitan city by its very nature, but it was immorality with a religious sanction. Corinth was full of prostitutes who were attached to the worship of Aphrodite. "Thousands of courtesans were attached to her temple. The worship of Aphrodite at Corinth was, like the worship of Artemis at Ephesus, an Eastern worship under a Greek name. What must have been the condition of a city, where such was the religion? . . . Corinth was the chosen resort of the vicious. A 'Corinthian' . . . was a synonym for a man of pleasure. . . . Indeed, sexual vice was there almost a matter of course. . . . To avoid the company of the vicious would be absolutely to go out of the world. . . ."[4] Such an environment had its effect on the church.

If the Corinthian Christians "were found to maintain that fornication was just as much a thing indifferent as the kind of food that was eaten (vi. 12–14),"[5] it is not surprising to find that problems concerning marriage arose in their minds. So they sent some of the questions to the Apostle Paul, whose answer is recorded in I Corinthians 7. We must remember that no copy of the questions which occasioned this reply exists. We are reading one side of a correspondence, or, to draw an analogy, listening to one side of a telephone conversation. Furthermore, the apostle himself states that some of his remarks at least were for the specific emergency,[6] but what that emergency was we do not know. In addition, it is plain that he is not writing a full treatise on marriage or even discussing the characteristics of the ideal married life. And yet even from this limited treatment a number of points bearing on the status of women are clear.

1. Paul does not say anything that would give the idea that he shared the view that marriage was to be avoided because it was polluting or evil in itself.[7] Some at Corinth were evidently urging the prohibition of all sexual relations, even those within the sphere of legal marriage. Where did such an idea arise? Dobschütz correctly answers:

To understand this line of thought, we must clearly realise that the ancient world as a whole saw something supernatural, something demoniacal in the act of generation. Sometimes it was deified—as in the Phrygian cults, the cult of the Phoenician Astarte, and the Aphrodite cults influenced by it; sometimes it was held on this very ground to be pollution. The idea of the Mosaic law that copulation causes one day's levitical pollution was widely spread in heathendom. . . . It is quite conceivable that this idea found support in the young Christian community of this city of excesses. In view of the immorality dominant in heathendom, and the ceremonial fostering which it received, every earnest moral movement was constrained to urge the other extreme of perfect abstinence within as well as without the marriage state, the renunciation of marital relations, and a vow of chastity on the part of the single.[8]

In his treatment of this matter Paul makes it perfectly clear that there is nothing impure about marriage; rather, it is even more desirable in the cases of the Corinthians "because of fornications," *dia tas porneias*.[9] Furthermore, suspension of sexual relations must not take place without mutual consent of both partners, only for a spiritual purpose, and only for a temporary period of time.[10]

2. Paul distinctly believed in a certain equality in the marriage relationship. The equality spoken of in verses 3 and 4 is restricted to sexual matters; nevertheless it is a Pauline dictum of equality which usually goes unnoticed. Of this "elegant paradox"[11] Findlay says, "The precise repetition of *omoiōs de kai* corrects the onesidedness of common sentiment and of public law,—both Greek and Jewish: *she* is as much the mistress of his person, as *he* the master of hers."[12]

3. The standards of Christianity allow no room for extra-marital relations. Beyond all doubt this greatly elevated the status of women above that which they had in the Greek world. Again it is Dobschütz whose words are apropos:

We are accustomed (or ought to be) to look upon adultery and fornication as equally sinful. The Grecian world of that time had quite another view. The respectable wife of a citizen brought up in strict seclusion remained shut up in her special apartments almost like an oriental, and in her case adultery hardly ever occurred. But on the streets hetairae were continually moving about in crowds, and they practised unchastity as "hierodules" in the service of a heathen temple. A man's intercourse with them, whether he was married or unmarried, was hardly reckoned any offence at all. In addition to this we must add the specific vice of that age, the sodomy, which had eaten its way so far into human thought as to have found philosophical justification. All this Christianity opposed with an inexorable "Thou shalt not commit adultery." But its insistence on moral purity met among the Christians of Corinth with the most vigorous opposition.[13]

4. In this chapter Paul gives celibacy the preference over marriage:

For I would that all men were even as I myself. . . . I say therefore to the unmarried and widows, It is good for them if they abide even as I. . . . Art thou loosed from a wife? seek not a wife. . . . But this I say, brethren, the time is short: it remaineth, that both they that have wives be as though they had none. . . . But I would have you without carefulness. He that is unmarried careth for the things that belong to the Lord, how he may please the Lord: But he that is married careth for the things that are of the world, how he may please his wife. . . . So then he that giveth her in marriage doeth well; but he that giveth her not in marriage doeth better. . . . But she is happier if she so abide, after my judgment.[14]

Whether or not Paul was married is not known, but plainly he was not married when he wrote these words, and he considered the celibate life a gift, a *charisma*. What reasons can we find for this decided preference for celibacy at least in the cases of Corinthian Christians? One has already been suggested; that is, that it was due to a reaction from the rampant immorality in the heathen society of Corinth. The teachings of Christ, known to these Christians, is a second reason which contributed to this preference for celibacy, for it was the Lord who said, "But woe to them that are with child, and to them that give suck in those days!" [15] Two other reasons are suggested by Paul himself in his discussion of the subject. One had to do with Christian hope and the other with Christian service.

The Christian's hope was in the personal return of his Saviour, which was expected shortly. In his discussion Paul points out that the time is short and that even those who are married should be as though they were not—not however by withdrawing from the world, but by using it with the awareness that it would soon pass away.[16] Such ideas are not exclusive to this passage, for one may easily see that many of the writers of the New Testament felt that they were living in a unique period of human history, the period which would see the portentous events surrounding the second coming of Christ. This idea "pervades most of the New Testament in one form or another, and its influence on ethical ideas must have been considerable." [17] Although the early Christians did not fully understand all that was involved, their sense of the impact of the other world and of the shortness of the time threw present living into a new light. This preference for celibacy is one of the best examples of how that worked, for "where the sense of impending catastrophe was strong, everything in this world seemed temporary and provisional; only things which would survive the passing of heaven and earth were worthy of attention." [18] Married life, of course, was not one of those things.[19]

How did this view of the future affect the status of women? Certainly this preference for celibacy was not asceticism, and Paul cannot be justly accused of being an ascetic in the sense of one who withdraws from the world; yet this preference was no doubt a precursor of asceticism. But actually asceticism gave woman a more exalted place, for it gave her an independence and prominence which she did not have before. It is not a big step from the preference for celibacy in I Corinthians to the rise of orders of virgins and deaconesses.

The fourth reason why celibacy is preferred is for the sake of the Lord's work.[20] Actually, this seems to be the most important reason in his mind, for even Paul's eschatological motives are pre-eminently practical. That the time is short means that the work is urgent, and it is the work that is of primary importance. Therefore, if more work can be accomplished by a single person, then celibacy is certainly to be preferred. But even if there were no eschatological factor, the urgency of getting the Lord's work done alone makes celibacy preferred. It is important for Christians today to remember that this is still a valid motive and was not something for the then "present emergency." Thus this chapter cannot be written off as an interim ethic. Doubtless many things in it were of an interim nature, but the emphasis on serving the Lord without distraction is valid as long as there is Christian work to be done. This writer agrees that the application of this teaching today is this:

If a person wishes to abstain from marriage that he may wholly devote himself to the work of the Lord, he must have these qualifications: steadfastness of purpose, freedom from any carnal obligations to marry, freedom from civil restraints, a genuine desire in his inmost heart as opposed to the promptings of another. Whoever abstains from domestic joys and sorrows in order to serve the Lord without distraction, and does not infringe any of these conditions, not only does not sin, but even does well.[21]

As to its first century significance, this teaching certainly implies that women may be engaged in the Lord's work with a certain equality with men, for throughout these verses Paul carefully balances the terminology used in connection with husbands and wives and in connection with unmarried men and virgins.[22] The unmarried Jewish woman was a reproach; the unmarried woman in ancient Greece was a woman of the street; the unmarried woman in Christianity could be a wholly dedicated and useful servant of her Lord.

5. Divorce among Christians is not allowed in the teaching of this chapter. We have seen that the Lord's teaching did not allow for divorce at all, which was a great advance over the practice of the Greeks and Romans and Jews. Paul reiterates this in the case of Christians, and he makes it clear that he is simply following the teaching of the Lord, for he did not command "but the Lord, Let

not the husband put away his wife." [23] "Had S. Paul held that adultery dissolved marriage or made its dissolution permissible, thus leaving either one or both parties free to contract a fresh union, would he not have said so?" [24] In cases of spiritually mixed marriages, where the mixture occurred after the marriage, the problems are more complex, but Paul's advice is that the believer is not to seek divorce, yet if the unbelieving partner insists upon it the believer cannot refuse. Nowhere, however, in such cases does Paul imply that the believer is free to marry again. Remarriage is allowed only after the death of one partner.[25] These standards are far superior to the best in heathen circles of that day, and they give protection to the rights of women. In addition, a genuine love and concern in marriage, which was not found among the heathen, is assumed in Christian wedlock even if it be a spiritually mixed one.

6. Virgins are under parental control. There are two principal interpretations of the verses concerning virgins.[26] The one understands simply a father-daughter relationship in which the father exercises moral judgment and authority over the marriageability of his daughter.[27] The important point of this interpretation is the matter of parental control. Not only is the father evidently the head of the Christian household, but he is also given rather stringent control over his children. The second interpretation, which is highly conjectural, sees here the first order of virgins.[28] Conceivably this teaching concerning celibacy might have been one of the contributing factors in a later rise of an order of virgins; that the order is in evidence here reads too much into the passage. Others continuing this line of reasoning see here the same sort of "spiritual marriage" which was practiced in the days of Cyprian.[29] However, the best understanding of the passage is simply that this is a word to fathers regarding their daughters, and it shows us how much they were controlled in Christian homes.

A summary of this section concerning marriage, celibacy, and related matters has revealed the following: (1) St. Paul did not entertain any idea that marriage was in itself evil; (2) there is an equality of the rights of each partner over the other; (3) Christianity does not countenance any extra-marital relations; (4) celibacy is preferred because of the shortness of the time and because of the work to be done; (5) divorce among Christians is not allowed; and (6) virgin daughters are under the control of their parents. Actually, all but the last point tended in some way to elevate the status of women in the Christian church.

HUSBAND-WIFE RELATIONSHIP

Though the Pauline authorship of Ephesians has been doubted, the trend today even among less conservative scholars is to accept it.[30] The traditional date which places its writing during the Roman captivity has also been argued for convincingly in recent years, though it, too, has been challenged.[31] However, if one accepts the Pauline authorship during the Roman captivity of Ephesians 5 and the Petrine authorship of I Peter 3, then, of course, these two passages were written about the same time. Selwyn, who puts the case for Petrine authorship as well as it has ever been put in the English language, suggests that the similarities in these two passages may be accounted for by the common use of some primitive Christian catechism which was at the disposal of all the early apostolic preachers.[32] To argue for or against this is beside the point here. Nevertheless, to believe that such might have been the case is certainly not to deny verbal inspiration in any sense.

Two ideas dominate these passages. One is the distinctively Christian ideal that love is to be the chief ingredient of marriage. St. Paul elevates this love to the very highest level when he says, "Husbands, love your wives, even as Christ also loved the church, and gave himself for it."[33] St. Peter enumerates two reasons for expecting such love when he states, "Likewise, ye husbands, dwell with them according to knowledge, giving honour unto the wife, as unto the weaker vessel, and as being heirs together of the grace of life; that your prayers be not hindered."[34] Such a standard of love was not found in Greek society, and the comparing of the love of a Christian husband and wife with the self-sacrificing love of Christ along with the Christian insistence on monogamy surpasses the standards of Judaism.

The other dominant idea in these two passages is the idea of subordination of the wife to the husband. Paul finds the reason for this submission in the headship of the husband, and Peter illustrates it by commending the example of Sarah who obeyed Abraham and called him lord. That subordination was widely taught in the early church is clear enough, especially if there be any truth to Selwyn's idea that this was a part of an early catechism. What it means, though, is not clear in the minds of most Christians today, for many immediately rebel as soon as the word is mentioned. One feels that another has written so well and with such balance and insight on this matter of subordination that his words must be quoted in full:

Subordination is entirely different from subjection or inferiority. St. Paul's doctrine as to the position of women is a doctrine of their subjection. . . . There is something slavish about [the associations of the word subjection], something which seems to speak of an inferior race held down by a stronger. But St. Paul's view of women is not this. . . . Now subordination is one thing, and inferiority is altogether another. . . . How can a Christian ever be guilty of confusing subordination with inferiority? What did his Lord and Master but take "the form of a servant, being made in the likeness of men," and become "obedient even unto death" not only to His Father in heaven, but to Joseph and Mary in their place, and even to those "meaner miserable," the rulers of His day? Did He regard Himself as inferior because He was subordinate? . . .

What then exactly is St. Paul's fundamental teaching on the question before us? He holds that within the Church, as well as without it, woman is meant to render obedience to her husband. She is to render it, not because she is inferior, but because he is under the Lord her appointed head. . . . The Apostle's point is that the principle of subordination prevails everywhere, and runs up into the life of heaven itself.[35]

In domestic relationships, then, God has appointed an order which includes the husband as the head and the wife in a place of honor though a place of subordination.

It must be remembered that whatever else may be considered

an "interim ethic" or for the "present distress," this teaching of subordination cannot be so considered, for it is based on the head-ship of Christ over His church which is an everlasting relationship. As long as the race continues and men are men and women women, then women are to be subject to their husbands as unto the head. This teaching is based on unalterable facts, and since the purpose of this chapter is to discover the domestic status of women in the early church, it is important to recognize this. The early church clearly considered the subordination of the wife in domestic relations the normal and fixed status.

QUESTIONS

1. What is Paul's teaching concerning marriage as revealed in I Corinthians 7? What parts of it are distinctive to the Christian message?

2. What does Paul teach about the subordination of the wife to her husband? Is this teaching applicable today?

NOTES

[1] I Corinthians 7.

[2] Ephesians 5:22–33.

[3] I Peter 3:1–7.

[4] H. L. Goudge, *The First Epistle to the Corinthians* (London, Methuen & Co., 1903), pp. xv–xvi.

[5] *Ibid.*, p. xvi.

[6] I Corinthians 7:26.

[7] I Corinthians 7:2, 28.

[8] Ernst von Dobschütz, *Christian Life in the Primitive Church* (London, Williams & Norgate, 1904), p. 40.

[9] I Corinthians 7:2.

[10] I Corinthians 7:5.

[11] John Albert Bengel, *Gnomon of the New Testament* (Edinburgh, T. & T. Clark, 1857), III, 244.

[12] G. G. Findlay, *First Corinthians, Expositor's Greek Testament* (London, Hodder & Stoughton, 1900), II, 822.

[13] *Op. cit.*, p. 44.

[14] I Corinthians 7:7, 8, 27, 29, 32, 33, 38, 40.

[15] Mark 13:17.

[16] I Corinthians 7:29–31.

[17] C. H. Dodd, *Gospel and Law* (New York, Columbia University Press, 1951), pp. 25–26.

[18] *Ibid.*, p. 28.

[19] Mark 12:25.

[20] I Corinthians 7:32–35.

[21] Thomas Charles Edwards, *The First Epistle to the Corinthians* (London, Hodder & Stoughton, 1885), p. 202.

[22] Cf. I Corinthians 7:32, 34.

[23] I Corinthians 7:10.

[24] Goudge, *op. cit.*, p. 55.

[25] I Corinthians 7:39.

[26] I Corinthians 7:36–38.

[27] Findlay, *op. cit.*, II, 836.

[28] Cf. Harnack, *The Mission and Expansion of Christianity*, II, 71–72, and Goudge, *op. cit.*, p. 62.

[29] Cf. H. Achelis, "Agapetae," *Encyclopaedia of Religion and Ethics* (Edinburgh, T. & T. Clark, 1908), I, 179.

[30] Cf. C. H. Dodd, *The Mind of Paul: Change and Development* (Manchester, Manchester University Press, 1934), p. 25, and Joseph Klausner, *From Jesus to Paul* (New York, Macmillan, 1944), p. 243.

[31] Again it is Dodd who aligns himself with the traditional date of Ephesians, *The Mind of Paul*, p. 26. In *The Epistle to the Ephesians* (Oxford, Clarendon Press, 1951), C. Leslie Mitton challenges this by suggesting that the epistle was written by a different author in the spirit of Paul but a generation after Paul, i.e., A.D. 87–92 (p. 261).

[32] Cf. Edward Gordon Selwyn, *The First Epistle of Saint Peter* (London, Macmillan, and New York, St. Martin's Press, 1946), pp. 363–466. "We conclude that . . . the New Testament authors were all writing on the basis of a catechetical pattern well known to their writers, and were developing it, each in his own way. The subjection of wives to their own husbands was certainly in the pattern, and it is probably enough that the pattern also included references to the need of conciliating public opinion and to modesty in woman's dress. In this case, however, it is St. Paul, not St. Peter, who develops the ethical theme into a great utterance of Christian theology, finding in the unity of man and wife and in the exclusiveness of their relationship a symbol of the unity between Christ and the Church" (p. 435).

[33] Ephesians 5:25.

[34] I Peter 3:7.

[35] Canon Goudge, "The Teaching of St. Paul as to the Position of Women," *The Place of Women in the Church* (London, Robert Scott, 1917), pp. 45–48.

Chapter VIII

THE PLACE OF WOMEN IN CHURCH LIFE

We have seen the important though secondary place which women played in the founding of the church and their position of subordination in domestic life. In this chapter we shall consider the role which women had in the public, official, and spiritual life of the Christian community.

Such a discussion should begin with St. Paul's great assertion of oneness in the body of Christ. Although the principle appears in several places in his writings,[1] it is only in the Galatian letter that it is applied to the relation between men and women. There he writes: "For ye are all the children of God by faith in Christ Jesus. For as many of you as have been baptized into Christ have put on Christ. There is neither Jew nor Greek, there is neither bond nor free, there is neither male nor female: for ye are all one in Christ Jesus."[2] Paul's meaning is clear, for he is speaking of the unity of all Christians in the body of the risen Lord, and in such a unity there can be no difference even in the status of male and female. The meaning is: the spiritual privileges in the body of Christ come equally to men and women.

There is an interesting comparison between the initiatory rites of Judaism and Christianity which illustrates this superior Christian equality of spiritual privilege. Even though both men and women were included in the Mosaic covenant, circumcision, which was originally given as a sign of the Abrahamic covenant and which later became one of the "chief symbols of the religion of Yahwe and of membership of the religious commonwealth,"[3] was limited to the males in the community. On the other hand, baptism, the symbol of acceptance of Christianity, is something that can be performed on men and women alike. Thus, Christianity's initiatory ordinance very vividly illustrates the principle of oneness in the body of Christ in which there is "neither male nor female," and it emphasizes the superiority of Christianity over Judaism. (Perhaps this may give a clue as to the reason the phrase "neither male nor female" appears only in the Galatian enunciation of this principle, since Judaising influences in those churches were tending to set up again the old distinctions.)

That this principle concerns spiritual privilege must be clearly understood. Unity of position and privilege does not mean uniformity of practice nor the obliteration of all differences between the sexes, and to use these words to imply that there can therefore be no subordination of women is to misunderstand Paul's meaning. If this were true, then clearly it would follow that neither could there be subordination of men to men, which would contradict all Scriptural teaching concerning principles and practices of church organization. Even Bishop Lightfoot, whose comment on this principle is so often misconstrued to mean that women can be allowed to do any sort of work in the church, recognized that unity does not mean uniformity, for his comment, if fully quoted, limited women's work. He said, "It is His call to you—you women-workers —to do a sister's part to these your sisters." [4]

It is clear, then, that Paul's words that in Christ there is neither male nor female include nothing that is inconsistent with the idea of a difference in position and function of men and women. By themselves, the words do not suggest what differences may exist, but at the same time they do not deny that they do exist. That the church considered the spiritual rights of women in the body of Christ to be equal with those of men is undeniable; but that the church considered the duties of each to be different is also undeniable and is the subject of investigation of the remainder of this chapter.

WOMEN IN PUBLIC WORSHIP

The activity of women "in the church," that is, in the public assemblies of Christians, is carefully regulated in the epistles of the

New Testament. The very fact that such regulations were needed shows how much women shared in the life of the early church. These regulations do not supersede but supplement the principle of equal privilege so clearly announced by Christianity, and they are found in such passages as these:

But I would have you know, that the head of every man is Christ; and the head of the woman is the man: and the head of Christ is God. Every man praying or prophesying, having his head covered, dishonoureth his head. But every woman that prayeth or prophesieth with her head uncovered dishonoureth her head: for that is even all one as if she were shaven.[5]

Let your women keep silence in the churches: for it is not permitted unto them to speak; but they are commanded to be under obedience, as also saith the law. And if they will learn any thing, let them ask their husbands at home: for it is a shame for women to speak in the church.[6]

But I suffer not a woman to teach, nor to usurp authority over the man, but to be in silence.[7]

The question of subordination. The first problem involved in these regulations is that of subordination of women to men in the public assembly. It centers in the use of the veil as indicated in I Corinthians 11, and it is one of the questions the Corinthians had written to Paul. Two factors probably contributed to the rise of this problem. One was the proclamation of spiritual equality which gave rise to an overemphasis on freedom. As Godet says: "Then there is no longer any difference, especially in worship, where we are all before God, between the demeanour of the male and that of the female. If the male speaks to his brethren or to God with his head uncovered, why should not the female do so also? And with the spirit of freedom which animated the Church of Corinth, it is not probable that they had stopped short at theory. They had already gone the length of practice; this seems to be implied by vers. 15, 16."[8]

The second factor was born of practical expediency. Women, no doubt, had exercised the gift of prophecy in the early days, for the Spirit of Pentecost could be poured out on daughters as well as on sons, on handmaidens as well as on bondmen.[9] Though there are almost no examples of the gift of prophecy being exercised by women in the New Testament, it is stated that Philip had four daughters who prophesied,[10] and the heretical prophetess Jezebel of Thyatira at least "tacitly presupposed that women could be, and actually were, prophetesses." [11] Since the church at Corinth lacked no spiritual gift,[12] it is not difficult to imagine that there were some women in that church who supposed that they had the gift and should be exercising it in public worship. It is easy to see what ran through their minds. "Very possibly the women had urged that, if the Spirit moved them to speak, they must speak; and how could they speak if their faces were veiled?" [13] It would be expedient, then, for women to come to church unveiled.

The answer to this problem is in certain respects only of secondary relevance to the purpose of this chapter in comparison to the principles which St. Paul employs in framing his answer. Goudge has well said:

It is noticeable, in the first place, that S. Paul regards this question as worth deciding, and does not brush it aside as trivial. There is a right, and a wrong, way of worshipping God. Secondly, he decided it by the touchstone of Christian doctrine. It is not a matter of taste; it is not a matter of national custom—S. Paul's decision runs counter to Jewish habit;—Christian ritual must conform to and express Christian doctrine, and on all points of importance doctrine will give the needed guidance. Thirdly, natural instincts of reverence and propriety must not be ruled out of court. And, fourthly, the duty of a local—S. Paul would no doubt add, of a national— church is to "hold fast the traditions" committed to it, and to see that it does not set at nought Apostolic practice and the custom of other churches.[14]

The importance of noticing that these regulations are an expression of Christian doctrine cannot be overemphasized, and the principal doctrine on which they are based is that of the subordina-

tion of women to men. Equality of spiritual privilege does not
nullify the principle of subordination which permeates the church,
and it was never in Paul's mind that it should. The same writer
under inspiration and without contradiction wrote "neither male
nor female" and "the head of the woman is the man." Neither
inferiority nor any deprivation of an immediate relation to the Lord
is implied, for Paul restates the principle of equality in the words,
"Nevertheless neither is the man without the woman, neither the
woman without the man, in the Lord." [15] At the same time the
position of the woman is a secondary one because she was created
out of the man.[16] The Christian doctrine of order in creation involving subordination requires the Christian practice of manifesting
that order in public worship by the veiling of women. "Before
man, the lord of creation, woman must have her head covered at
worship, since that is the proper way for her to recognize the divine
order at Creation." [17]

Paul's mention of the angels [18] confirms the importance of this
emphasis on order, for as Moffatt writes: "Paul has in mind the
midrash on Gen. i. 26 f., which made good angels not only mediators
of the Law (Gal. iii. 19), but guardians of the created order. . . .
They were specially present at worship; in his Greek Bible the
apostle read allusions to this, e.g. in Ps. cxxxviii. 1. . . ." [19] If angels
desire to look into things pertaining to salvation,[20] then they should
see as they look at veiled women in the assembly of Christians the
voluntary submission of a woman to her head. Thus the early church
(for this was the custom of the churches generally [21]) while offering
religious equality in spiritual privilege insisted on showing in public
worship the principle of subordination of women by their being
veiled.

The question of silence. Another problem concerns what vocal
ministry women exercised in the church. The solution to this problem involves among other things what appears to be a contradiction
in St. Paul's own teaching on this subject. In I Corinthians 11:5 he
seems clearly to imply that women may pray and prophesy in public
if veiled. Yet when discussing the subject of spiritual gifts and
especially the gift of tongues he apparently withdraws that limited

permission when he writes, "Let your women keep silence in the churches: for it is not permitted unto them to speak." [22] In the Pastorals he is equally emphatic in declaring that women are not to teach in the public assembly of the church.[23]

Many solutions have been suggested for this difficulty. Edwards simply says that the permission to pray and prophesy is withdrawn upon further reflection.[24] Findlay, placing weight on I Timothy 2:12, argues that praying and prophesying among women were part of their regular ministry and that the prohibition of I Corinthians 14 is against *"Church-teaching and authoritative direction as a role unfit for women."* [25] A more recent writer (and a woman) also defends the regularity of women's praying and prophesying but thinks that the prohibition is against unseemly hysterical outbursts which might occur from them in the excitement of men speaking in tongues. This, she says, was "called forth by special circumstances and never intended to be binding on all women or for all time." [26] All of these proposed solutions have one thing in common. They all place emphasis on the concession to praying and prophesying in I Corinthians 11 and, as it were, determine the meaning of the prohibition of Chapter 14 by that. As a consequence, when considering the prohibition of the Pastorals its value is deprecated as not representing the apostle's views. Thus Scott says:

The rule is laid down authoritatively in the name of the great apostle, but it is doubtful whether Paul would have expressed himself quite so strongly. He was indeed averse to women making themselves heard in the assembly (1 Cor. xiv. 35), but he by no means forbade them to teach. . . . Perhaps in the present passage the word teach is to be taken in the technical sense of making a set public address.[27]

But how can a woman teach without "making a set public address"? Miss Robbins follows in the same vein with no more success when she declares that the value of I Timothy 2:12 "as an expression of the apostle's commands is lessened when we remember that modern scholars consider this epistle to be the work of an earnest Paulinist early in the second century." [28] But if the Pastorals were not written by Paul, as some scholars think, and which fact Miss Robbins takes refuge in, would not the earnest Paulinist who supposedly did write them be more likely to represent than to misrepresent the mind of the apostle? In any case, even if he did not represent Paul's mind, he did represent the mind of some segment of the early church on this subject which believed that women should not teach. [29] Disbelieving the Pauline authorship of the Pastorals does not rid one of the problem of the clear prohibition.

Thus the solution is not found by placing the emphasis on the permission of Chapter 11 and making that determine how to interpret Chapter 14 and the Pastoral prohibition. Suppose the emphasis were shifted and placed on the prohibition of Chapter 14 rather than on the permission of Chapter 11. If so, the silence of women then becomes the general rule and the exercise of prayer and prophecy the exception. This shift of emphasis would be supported by the fact that between the time of the writing of I Corinthians and I Timothy there was a more careful defining of the ministry of women and it was in the direction of less public ministry. In his directions concerning public worship in I Timothy 2, Paul limits the exercise of leading in public prayer to men, for the use of the Greek word for male, *anēr*, [30] clearly places the responsibility of prayer in the church on males, and public prayer is evidently by the same token not a part of the good works which women are to perform. All of this indicates that even at the time of the writing of I Corinthians the exception was permitting women to speak in any capacity in public worship.

Further evidence for this solution which makes the prohibition the norm and the permission the exception is found in the literary context of I Corinthians. The point is simply this: the question which evoked the answer recorded in I Corinthians 11 concerned women's using the veil. Was it now necessary with the freedom and equality they now had in Christ? Paul was not dealing there with the question of women's praying and prophesying. The question which evoked the answer recorded in Chapter 14 was the question of the proper use of spiritual gifts. At this point in the epistle he was dealing with the question of the public ministry of women. In other words, Chapter 11 concerns women's position and Chapter 14 their activity in the public assembly. In the section which deals with principles governing the activity of women in public he declares that they should keep silent. This seems clearly to indicate that the emphasis should be put on the general prohibition of Chapter 14 which specifically deals with the question of ministry.

What, then, it will be asked, did Paul mean when he seemed to speak of women's praying and prophesying in I Corinthians 11:5? In general, one may answer that, in light of the general prohibition of Chapter 14 which was clearly the custom of all the churches, it appears that the fact that women prayed and prophesied at all was very extraordinary and probably limited to the Corinthian congregation. As has been pointed out, Corinth was a city of very loose standards, and although there were undoubtedly many women of good standing among the early converts in that city, just as surely there must have been many converts from the lower classes whose presence in the assembly would give rise to many problems. The obvious consequence is clearly seen by Dobschütz:

As usual, the freer and more progressive tendency gained more acceptance. Among the Libertines . . . emancipated women must have played an important part. They were evidently the least trustworthy element in the Church, the soul of the opposition against the Apostle, and his earnest discipline. He becomes impassioned whenever he has to speak of their "emancipation," which nothing could bring to reason. . . .[31]

When, therefore, Paul deals with the question of discarding the veil, he recognizes the fact that some women were accustomed to praying and prophesying in the assembly, but it does not necessarily follow that he approved of it. This is the very point which is overlooked. When he does come to the place in the epistle where he speaks his mind on that particular subject, he lays down a strict prohibition against women speaking at all. However, it is true that he does not condemn outright the exceptional case of a woman praying or prophesying as long as she is properly veiled, but the historical setting at Corinth supports the contention that such occurrences were unusual and limited to the Corinthian congregation. With this conclusion Godet substantially agrees, declaring in comparing these two passages in I Corinthians:

. . . we think we shall not be far from the apostle's view if we thus state that result of the two passages taken together: "As to women, if, under the influence of a sudden inspiration or revelation, they wish to take the work in the assembly to give utterance to a prayer or prophecy, I do not object; only let them not do so without having the face veiled. But in general, let women keep silence. For it is improper on their part to speak in church." [32]

Godet certainly puts the emphasis in the right place, but Robertson and Plummer go further by suggesting that the case of women praying and prophesying may be hypothetical:

They had been claiming equality with men in the matter of the veil, by discarding this mark of subjection in Church, and apparently they had also been attempting to preach, or at any rate had been asking questions during service. We are not sure whether St. Paul contemplated the *possibility* of women prophesying in exceptional cases. What is said in xi. 5 may be hypothetical. Teaching he forbids them to attempt; . . . a rule taken over from the synagogue and maintained in the primitive Church (1 Tim. ii. 12). [33]

Thus we conclude (and motivated, as some other writers cannot be, only by a desire to discover the early church's outlook on this matter without trying to defend any contemporary practice) that the early church did not make a practice of permitting women to speak in their public meetings. That it may have been done in prayer and prophesying cannot be absolutely denied in every case, but it was decidedly the exception and not the general practice. At Corinth it doubtless occurred more frequently because of the nature of the composition of the church, but even there Paul's governing principle is silence for women. That this teaching was widespread early in the church is evident from the repetition of it in the Pastorals.

Finally, it is important to notice that this principle of silence is linked to the principle of subjection and difference between the sexes and grounded in the Genesis account of creation and the fall.[34] In Paul's mind the principle of subjection is basic to that of silence and is a result of the fall of man and continues throughout the present economy. The important point is, of course, that Paul's basic principle was not something which was simply forged on the spur of the moment because of the particular situation in one local church of the first century. It is grounded in facts which are not altered by geography or centuries. Similarly in the Pastorals the rule of silence is linked with the account of creation. The fact that Adam was first formed means that he had first an independent existence and could in no way be subordinate to Eve. He further adds the idea that "the woman's yielding to the wiles of a serpent shows her to be an unsafe guide." [35] Subordination,[36] dependence,[37] and difference of nature [38] are the three reasons the early church assigned for the non-participation of women in public vocal ministry, and this regulation of silence was not grounded in special and temporary conditions in the church but was related to a far more basic and fundamental reason, that is, the difference in position and nature of male and female. These are the facts whether we like them or not, and this appears to be the only solution which makes all the texts consistent with one another. Whether this agrees with present-day practice is beside the point. Every serious student of the Word of God first seeks to discover its meaning and standards and then, and only then, to bring practice into conformity with it. Biblical principles determine Biblical practice, and the principle of silence was the principle of the first century church.

Lest the author be accused of saying something he did not say or of neglecting to say something he should have said, perhaps a word is in order concerning the relation of the preceding principles to present-day practice as it exists in many evangelical churches. I trust that it has been evident that my main concern has been to honor the Word of God by attempting to discover the correct interpretation of individual texts which will be consistent with one another. That should be every Christian's first desire regardless of any so-called consequences in the practical realm.

Actually, the solutions to the problems raised by this discussion are not so difficult as they are delicate. It is only too apparent that the early church did not allow its women to take part audibly in public worship. That included preaching, praying in mixed company, and teaching men in public. It is equally evident that they served in many other ways, but the questions today always revolve around their public ministry in the church. If the practice of the early church is authoritative by way of example for us today, then women should not lead in any way in public worship. This does not mean that a woman may not teach children, for this is definitely her God-given privilege, nor that she may not lead in prayer in women's groups or in teaching other women. However, she should not do even these things if they interfere in any way with her responsibilities toward her own children. She must never usurp the authority God gave to the man to lead in the public life of the church. This is the pattern established in Scripture.

However, we do not live in an ideal world. There are many times on both the home and foreign fields when there are simply no men to do the work. In such instances this writer feels that we need to remember that Paul not only commanded that things be done decently and in order but also that they be done. In such cases, then, one feels that it is better to do the work with qualified women—even though this is not ideal—than to sit back and do nothing simply because there are no men. However, women must be cautioned against continuing in such work after there are trained men available for the job. Any woman who finds herself doing a man's work should so aim her own work that a man can assume it as quickly as possible. The acid test any woman can apply to such situations is simply this: Would I be willing to give over all my work to a trained man if he should appear today? To know the Scriptural pattern is absolutely essential. To aim our labors toward attaining that ideal is the only practical way to serve in the present-day situation.

WIDOWS

The Old Testament often espouses the cause of the widow and orphan. God is spoken of as the judge of widows,[39] and the Mosaic law pronounced a special curse upon those who afflicted widows.[40] The *leviratus,* that is, the marriage of a widow by her brother-in-law after the death of her husband, helped protect the rights of a widow. However, even that law made provision for releasing the brother-in-law when there were circumstances that would produce hardship on him if he fulfilled his obligation.[41] As a result Levirate marriage was neglected, and widows, left to make their own way, became the objects of charity.[42] So neglected had they become at the time of Christ that the Jews had established a fund in the temple for the purpose of relief to widows and orphans.[43]

When some of these widows, who have been receiving support from the temple fund, were converted and joined the Christian community, the support they had been getting was naturally cut off, and the early Christians, who were also Jews, quite naturally assumed the responsibility of caring for them. Thus in the early record there appears a large group of widows supported by the church.[44] It is a natural, normal development from the Jewish background of the first Christians. It seems likely that the practice of giving relief to widows was begun shortly after Pentecost and continued smoothly for a few months until a murmuring arose because some felt that the distribution was not being done systematically. The murmuring resulted in further organization in the church, but not of organization of the widows, for as yet there certainly was no order of widows assigned any duties in the church but only a class which was recognized as needy.

The story of Dorcas further illustrates that widows as a class were prominent in other Christian communities.[45] It also indicates that these widows were nothing more than the recipients of relief and were not bound together in any sort of order—the only bond being their common need. That Dorcas herself was a widow need not be assumed. Luke's probable meaning is that she devoted herself to charitable work and that the widows who came to lament over her body were those who had profited from her work. Dorcas was probably instructed to do such work by her knowledge of the Old Testament and the example of Jesus,[46] and these would be sufficient motives to account for the naturalness of the account in Acts. The story further emphasizes the fact that there is no record of the widows' ministering in any way to the church in return for the relief given them. There was no order at that time.

The *locus classicus*, however, concerning widows in the New Testament is I Timothy 5:3–16. By the time that Paul wrote this epistle in the mid-sixties, provision was made for a definite order of widows with specific requirements for admission. There are problems, however, in the passage, and they center in two questions: (1) What was the purpose of the enrolling? and (2) What duties, if any, did the widows have in relation to the church?

Some of the confusion and vagueness of the commentaries might be dissipated if the principal subject of the passage were kept in the fore. The subject which Paul is discussing is the relief of widows. Any service to be performed in return, any enrolling, any qualifications are all secondary to this principal theme. Obviously the church had continued to support widows from the early days, but with the passing of time certain abuses had arisen. One of these was that relatives of widows were not assuming their own responsibilities toward their widows but rather were pushing the matter of support onto the church. So Paul twice admonishes relatives to be responsible for those widows in their own families. In the first instance the admonition concerns younger unenrolled widows, while in the second it evidently related to enrolled ones.[47] The second, then, is not a mere repetition of the first, for "since *v.*9 the whole thought has been of enrolled widows, who do not include all necessitous widows. Here then it is a question also of enrolled widows: some of them would be well to do and able to support themselves, some necessitous. Of the latter class, some would have relations able to support them, and, in that case, though the widows are doing Church work, they are supported by their relations: others would have no such relations and are to be supported by the Church." [48] The first clear principle, then, in regard to widows' relief is that relatives must assume their support whenever possible.

The second principle is that the church must support those who are unable to be supported by relatives. "Widows indeed," *ontōs chērai,* or "real widows" are not, as many commentators seem to suggest, to be defined as the enrolled widows. They are defined in the Scripture as those who are desolate, trusting in God, and continuing in prayers day and night.[49] Financial and family status, not age, is the primary qualification for a "widow indeed." It cannot be assumed, therefore, that enrolled widows were the only ones who had a claim upon the church for its charity. *Tima* clearly means material support, and the plain injunction to honor "widows indeed" is given before the word about enrolling.[50] "It cannot be supposed . . . that the Church would refuse help to a widow if she was under sixty, for this restriction would be simply cruel if the question were one of charity; the widows in direst need would generally be the younger ones, who were left with small children." [51] On the other hand, to say that the enrolling was entirely unrelated to material need is to miss the point also, for it is clear that, unless they had relatives who could support them, enrolled widows were in some way the special charge of the church. Therefore, the best we can say is that financial need is related to enrolling for those over sixty but not determinative of enrolling, since the church undoubtedly gave relief also to younger unenrolled widows.

The second question, as stated in the opening paragraph of this section, concerns what ministry widows may have had. It is clear and agreed by all that they did have a ministry of prayer and supplication for the church,[52] but it is not agreed as to what additional ministry they may or may not have had. Scott, for instance, is sure that the enrolling was indicative of "certain duties the Church required" of them because they "could be counted on to devote themselves wholly to the work." [53] However, there are two objections to saying that the enrolled widows were those who were engaged in some sort of work. The first is well stated thus:

. . . it is difficult to suppose that St. Paul, or any other practically minded administrator, would contemplate a presbyteral order of widows, the members of which would enter on their duties at the age of 60, an age relatively more advanced in the East and in the first century than in the West and in our own time.[54]

The second objection is that if the ministry may be presumed to be related to the going from house to house, then obviously the younger unenrolled widows were also engaged in it and were abusing their privilege—thus calling forth the restriction.[55] Ewald makes a suggestion as to what the ministry might have been. He thinks that widows went from house to house collecting money for the needs of the church.[56] More clearly, however, verse 10 shows that widows (and it applies to younger unenrolled widows too) may have been responsible for the rearing of orphan children. This may have been part of their ministry to the Christian community in addition to that of prayer; but whatever it was or was not, it is clear that any actual ministry was not limited to enrolled widows.

To sum up: (1) relief by the church was not limited to enrolled widows, though it was assumed in the cases of all enrolled widows except those who may have had relatives to support them; (2) the ministry of prayer was expected of all "widows indeed" regardless of age, and any other ministries which may be suggested by the text were not limited to enrolled widows. What, then, was the purpose of the catalogue of widows over sixty who met certain requirements? That it meant financial support by the church in every needy case is clear. That it meant a special ministry by those enrolled which was not performed by those unenrolled is not supported by the passage. Official support was part of the enrolling; official duties were not. The catalogue was instituted to correct and systematize financial matters, and no doubt it paved the way for the development of orders of ministry among women, but at this point in history matters are still undefined. "There are more detailed regulations for the qualifications of a widow than there were for bishop or deacon, as if the order were not yet fully established."[57]

In the attempt to unravel the threads of thought concerning the order of widows, one must not neglect to notice three other facts in this section which bear on the status of women. (1) It is evident that widows were accorded a place of honor in the early church, and they were the first group of women to be honored in any way as a group. (2) Younger women are advised to marry, and no preference was given to celibacy. (3) The work of women is still primarily connected with the home. "I will therefore that the younger women marry, bear children, guide the house, give none occasion to the adversary to speak reproachfully." [58]

DEACONESSES

In reality the position of deaconesses in the New Testament is not so clearly or easily defined as that of women in public worship or even that of widows. Harnack seems to understand Pliny's mention of the two *ministrae* in his letter to Trajan to be the first reference to deaconesses as any sort of recognized group in the church.[59] Lightfoot, on the other hand, is emphatic in declaring that deaconesses did comprise an order in New Testament times. He says: "The Apostolic Church had its organized ministries of women—its order of deaconesses and its order of widows. Women had their definite place in the ecclesiastical system of those primitive times." [60] In another place he declares: "As I read my New Testament, the female diaconate is as definite an institution in the Apostolic Church as the male diaconate. Phoebe is as much a deacon as Stephen or Philip is a deacon." [61] Obviously, with such divergence of viewpoint additional investigation is in order. Unfortunately, the evidence is scanty, for there are only two verses in the entire New Testament which shed any light on this subject.[62]

We have already seen how women served (*diakoneō*) Christ. The seven chosen by the church in Jerusalem served tables (*diakonein trapexais*).[63] Others who served and either to whom or to whose service *diakonos* or *diakonia* is applied include Paul,[64] Stephanas,[65] Archippus,[66] Timothy,[67] Apollos,[68] and Epaphras.[69] *Diakonos* is used with such wide meaning that it includes the work of our Lord [70] and that of governments.[71] It is the most general term used for all kinds of ministry, and in this general sense there is of course a male and female diaconate in the New Testament. The real question is, however, Did it come to be used in an official sense to designate a special group with certain functions? The general or unofficial use of the word is easily recognized, but the problems concerning an official diaconate and the relation of women to it are far more complicated.

It has generally been considered that official deacons were first chosen to settle the dispute over the relief of widows in the Jerusalem church.[72] However, Vitringa was quite right in calling attention years ago to the fact that these seven men were not deacons in the official sense.[73] In a more recent work A. M. Farrer calls these men the first non-apostolic elders,[74] while Gregory Dix puts it this way:

There were subordinate duties to be fulfilled towards the Christian society as a society, not easily included under *episkopē*—"superintendence,"—and those who performed these habitually come to be charged with them. In the course of a generation the performance of the duty hardens into a distinct office.[75]

Thus one could not conclude that there existed even an official male diaconate in the first years of the life of the church.

It is clear that by the time that Paul wrote to the Philippians there was in that church an order of deacons who were distinguished from the elders.[76] Yet at the same time *diakonos* continued to be used in its general, unofficial sense.[77] By the time of the writing of the Pastorals the diaconate was a well-established and distinct body,[78] and yet during the same period the word was used in that general sense.[79] Therefore, during the first century ministry in general was called "deaconing," while during the same period the official diaconate was developing into a distinctly recognized group in the church.

The question concerning Phoebe, who is commended as a *diakonon* of the church which is at Cenchrea, is actually a question

of whether *diakonos* is used in the general, unofficial sense of ministering in any way or in the more restricted use in connection with
an established diaconate. Lightfoot is certain that Phoebe was an
official deacon of that church.[80] Godet, too, declares that the phrase
"servant of the Lord" means "invested with an ecclesiastical office." [81]
No one questions the need in the early church for women workers.
As Lightfoot points out, "The strict seclusion of the female sex in
Greece and in some Oriental countries necessarily debarred them
from the ministrations of men: and to meet the want thus felt, it
was found necessary at an early date to admit women to the diaconate." [82] Neither is there any doubt that Phoebe rendered important services to the church, but whether this coupled with the
need furnishes sufficient evidence of an order of deaconesses is not
proved. Linguistics and chronology bear heavily on solving the
problem.

The linguistic consideration concerns Phoebe's designation as a
prostatis pollōn. Indeed, this is the strongest argument for Phoebe's
being an official of the church at Cenchrea. In the New Testament
proistēmi includes the idea of governing in the church,[83] and in some
instances it concerns official duties. All the New Testament references include to a greater or lesser extent the idea of having authority or presiding either in the family or over oneself.[84] The meaning
then ranges from simple presiding to definite ruling.

Extra-Biblical evidence throws further light on the meaning of
prostatis. Although they do not cite any instance of the use of the
feminine form, Moulton and Milligan note that the masculine
prostatēs is a title which "is applied to the office-bearer in a heathen
religious association." [85] In Judaism the word was used in an unofficial sense, for Josephus describes King David as *"prostatēn te
kai kēdemona genous tōn Hebraiōn,"* protector and guardian of the
Hebrew race.[86] Juster points out further that:

The President of the council was called, as often as not, gerusiarch,
but sometimes, also *epistatēs tōn palaiōn* or *prostatēs.* In the metro-
politan cities this Presidency was exercised by the chief Jew of the

province, that is, by the little patriarch. Elsewhere it was the chief religious person—the archisynagogos—who, as often as not, had this presidency.[87]

Schürer is quite definite also in declaring that in the age of the procurators (A.D. 44–66) the high priest who held the presidency of the sanhedrim was called *prostatēs tou ethnous,* and although these high priests were set up and removed at the pleasure of the Roman procurator, nevertheless they did have governmental functions.[88]

How should this evidence be evaluated in the case of Phoebe? The mere fact that she is called a "deacon" does not necessarily imply an order of deaconesses, for, as will be shown, the term is still non-technical at this time in the history of the church. But the fact that she is called a succorer, *prostatis,* is significant, for even in its most non-technical sense the word implies active and important functions. The question is, How technical is its meaning in this instance? Did Phoebe's service include ruling in the church as an office-bearer? I feel that this is an unwarranted conclusion for two reasons. First, although *prostatēs* does imply official ruling, there is not a single instance of a woman holding such an office (unless, of course, Phoebe herself be the single instance, but such an exception from the Bible would be strange in view of the fact that there is no extra-Biblical exception). Second, although honorary titles of the synagogue were conferred on women for outstanding service (usually charity), these titles had no official significance. Again Phoebe would have to be the lone exception unless her title is simply one of honor without carrying with it an official position. Actually, the very fact that she is called by a title which is linked to the eldership in other places but which here is linked with a supposed diaconate seems to reinforce my contention that both titles, succorer and deaconess, are used in an unofficial sense. However, one must concede that even in its unofficial sense *prostatis* includes some kind of leadership, but I believe that there is no idea of rulership in it in Phoebe's case. What sort of leading did Phoebe do? Sanday and Headlam suggest that the leadership she exercised was largely financial and social. In other words, her wealth and social position in the community enabled her "to act as patroness of a small and struggling community." [89] Her activity was important to this small church, and certainly her importance and influence are not to be disparaged in any way; but to see in Phoebe evidence for an established order of deaconesses or for female officials in the church is to see more than the evidence warrants.

In addition to the linguistic evidence there is also an argument from the chronology which confirms the conclusion that though women had important duties there was not yet an ecclesiastical order of deaconesses. Another has so well stated the argument that it is reproduced here in full:

On the other hand, since there is not in the two earlier groups of Paul's epistles any other indication that *diakonia* is a special office in the Church, this, which occurs in the second group, would be a solitary and somewhat puzzling exception. Moreover, as Cenchreae was the E. port of Corinth, this case practically belongs to the Corinthian church. In that church special mention is made of the *diakonia* of Stephanas and his household, the word *diakonia* being used in its broadest sense. There also Chloe and her household were of note. It may be, therefore, that Phoebe was another woman of influence who held a corresponding pre-eminence of service in the neighbouring port, a pre-eminence that earned for her at the apostle's hands the honourable title of *diakonos* of the church; for she had been a helper . . . of many and of the apostle himself. If we could assume that the diaconate was formally established in the Corinthian church at this time, we should certainly conclude that Phoebe was one of the women who served it; but this assumption is in sharp contrast with the silence of Paul's epistles as to any kind of definite ecclesiastical organization at Corinth.

Of Phoebe, then, we may say with security that she is a witness of the important services rendered by women in the primitive Church; but in tracing the history of the diaconate it will not be wise to assume that the word *diakonos* is used of her in the strictly official sense. [90]

Thus we conclude that the first reference, Romans 16:1, the case of Phoebe, does not present evidence of an order of deaconesses at that time in the church.

In the second passage, I Timothy 3:11, where in the context we meet more fully developed ecclesiastical organization, qualifications are given for elders, for deacons, and for *gunaikas*. The problem has been obscured by the Authorized Version's translation *wives* (of the deacons), for actually the Greek word only means women, which might mean wives of deacons or some sort of women workers, even possibly deaconesses. The great majority of commentators seem to understand the reference to be to deaconesses.[91] The view is supported by the obvious fact that there was a need for women workers, and one would expect to find them listed along with other church officials. Further, the omission of any reference to wives of the elders would indicate that these women are not the wives of deacons. But such a view almost necessitates suggesting that verse 11 is out of place because the following verse reverts to qualifications for deacons. It would be very difficult for anyone to prove that the verse is out of order, and impossible for this author to believe. No one denies the necessity for having women workers, but one must be on guard against reading back into the New Testament subsequent development in church organization. Further, the writing of I Timothy was not many years after that of Romans, which fact (if it be true that there were no deaconesses in Romans) does not help the argument that these women were deaconesses. So in view of these considerations about the context, it would not be wise to assume that these women were official deaconesses.

What, then, can we say about these women? The need for women workers was there, and women did play an active role in the life of the early church even though they did not assume places of leadership. If deacons were concerned with the physical and material needs of the community, what would be unnatural about their wives sharing in these ministries as they concerned other women?[92] This accounts for what otherwise would be an intrusion of verse 11 into the discussion about deacons. Further, if a specific class of women workers was established by this time, then why did not Paul use a more specific designation? *Diakonos* with the feminine article or *diakonissa* would probably have come to his mind if this had been the case. That these women were a female diaconate is an assumption; that these women ministered and actually did the work of a *diakonos*, used in its general sense, is quite evident. At Ephesus the particular group of women who were active in this manner were the wives of deacons; at Cenchrea it was only one woman, Phoebe. Or at least she was the outstanding one. But that there was any official body of deaconesses, in the sense in which the term has come to stand for an organization, in the New Testament is untenable. Women workers, yes; women deacons, no.

QUESTIONS

1. How is the woman's use of the veil in church related to the doctrine of her subordination?

2. Should a woman keep silent in public worship? How do you interpret I Corinthians 11:5 in relation to I Corinthians 14:34?

3. If the Scriptural ideal is that women should be silent in public worship, how can you work toward that ideal in your own church?

4. How did the early church care for her widows?

5. Is there evidence that an official order of deaconesses existed in New Testament days? Who are the women mentioned in I Timothy 3:11 and what did they do for the church?

NOTES

[1] Romans 10:12; I Corinthians 12:13; Colossians 3:11.
[2] Galatians 3:26–28.
[3] Immanuel Benzinger, "Circumcision," *Encyclopaedia Biblica* (New York, Macmillan, 1914), p. 831.
[4] Joseph Barber Lightfoot, *Sermons Preached on Special Occasions* (London, Macmillan, 1891), p. 222.
[5] I Corinthians 11:3–5.
[6] I Corinthians 14:34–35.
[7] I Timothy 2:12.
[8] F. Godet, *First Epistle to the Corinthians* (Edinburgh, T. & T. Clark, 1887), II, 105.
[9] Acts 2:17–18.
[10] Acts 21:9.
[11] Harnack, *The Mission and Expansion of Christianity*, II, 69.

[12] I Corinthians 1:7.

[13] Archibald Robertson and Alfred Plummer, *First Epistle of St Paul to the Corinthians, International Critical Commentary* (Edinburgh, T. & T. Clark, 1911), p. 230.

[14] Goudge, *The First Epistle to the Corinthians,* p. 97.

[15] I Corinthians 11:11.

[16] I Corinthians 11:8.

[17] James Moffatt, *The First Epistle of Paul to the Corinthians, Moffatt New Testament Commentary* (London, Hodder & Stoughton, 1938), p. 153.

[18] I Corinthians 11:10.

[19] *Op. cit.,* p. 152.

[20] I Peter 1:12.

[21] This is the meaning of I Corinthians 11:16.

[22] I Corinthians 14:34.

[23] I Timothy 2:12.

[24] Thomas Charles Edwards, *The First Epistle to the Corinthians* (London, Hodder & Stoughton, 1885), p. 381.

[25] *First Corinthians,* II, 915.

[26] Irene M. Robbins, "St. Paul and the Ministry of Women," *Expository Times,* XLIV, No. 4 (January, 1935), 186.

[27] E. F. Scott, *The Pastoral Epistles, Moffatt New Testament Commentary* (London, Hodder & Stoughton, 1936), p. 26.

[28] *Op. cit.,* p. 185.

[29] Cf. P. N. Harrison, *The Problem of the Pastoral Epistles* (Oxford, Oxford University Press, 1921), p. 9: "[The writer] believed honestly and wholeheartedly the Pauline gospel as he understood it. At the same time he shared the ideas of the Church of his own day on matters both of belief and of polity. . . . Of this difference, however, from original Pauline conceptions, the writer himself was no more aware than were his contemporaries. He and they regarded themselves as simply holding on to the genuine apostolic teaching."

[30] I Timothy 2:8–9.

[31] *Christian Life in the Primitive Church,* p. 37.

[32] *Op. cit.,* II, 313–314.

[33] *Op. cit.,* pp. 324–325.

[34] I Corinthians 14:34; I Timothy 2:13–14; Genesis 3:16.

[35] R. St John Parry, *The Pastoral Epistles* (Cambridge, Cambridge University Press, 1920), p. 15.

[36] I Corinthians 14:34.

[37] I Timothy 2:13.

[38] I Timothy 2:14.

[39] Psalm 68:5.

[40] Deuteronomy 27:19.

[41] Deuteronomy 25:7–10; Ruth 4:4–10.

[42] Deuteronomy 24:19; 26:12–13.

[43] II Maccabees 3:10.

[44] Acts 6:1–7.

[45] Acts 9:36–41.

[46] Proverbs 31; Matthew 6:2–4.

[47] I Timothy 5:4, 16.

[48] Parry, *op. cit.,* p. 31.

[49] I Timothy 5:5.

[50] I Timothy 5:3.

[51] Scott, *op. cit.*, p. 60.

[52] I Timothy 5:5.

[53] *Loc. cit.*

[54] Newport J. D. White, *The First Epistle to Timothy, Expositor's Greek Testament* (London, Hodder & Stoughton, 1910), IV, 130.

[55] I Timothy 5:13.

[56] Heinrich Ewald, *The History of Israel* (London, Longmans, Green & Co., 1878), VIII, 202.

[57] Walter Lock, *The Pastoral Epistles, International Critical Commentary* (Edinburgh, T. & T. Clark, 1924), p. 56.

[58] I Timothy 5:14.

[59] *Op. cit.*, I, 122n.

[60] *Sermons Preached on Special Occasions*, p. 226.

[61] *Primary Charge* (London, Macmillan, n.d.), p. 33. Those who appeal to Lightfoot for authority to allow women to exercise any type of ministry should note his further word: "We may find some difficulty in defining the precise line where S. Paul's prohibition (1 Cor. xiv. 34), as interpreted in the light of other passages (1 Cor. xi. 5), fixes the limits of the woman's function as a religious teacher; but in the philanthropic and charitable work of the Church, which is her proper sphere, her capabilities are inexhaustible."

[62] Romans 16:1; I Timothy 3:11.

[63] Acts 6:2.

[64] Acts 20:24; Ephesians 3:7.

[65] I Corinthians 16:15.

[66] Colossians 4:17.

[67] I Timothy 4:6; II Timothy 4:5.

[68] I Corinthians 3:5.

[69] Colossians 1:7.

[70] Galatians 2:17.

[71] Romans 13:4.

[72] Acts 6:1–7.

[73] *De Synagoga Vetere*, p. 914.

[74] Kenneth E. Kirk, editor, *The Apostolic Ministry* (London, Hodder & Stoughton, 1946), p. 143.

[75] *Ibid.*, p. 244.

[76] Philippians 1:1.

[77] Colossians 1:7.

[78] I Timothy 3:8–10.

[79] I Timothy 4:6.

[80] J. B. Lightfoot, *Dissertations on the Apostolic Age* (London, Macmillan, 1892), p. 148.

[81] F. Godet, *Commentary on St. Paul's Epistle to the Romans* (Edinburgh, T. & T. Clark, 1881), II, 386.

[82] *Loc. cit.*

[83] I Timothy 5:17; Romans 12:8; I Thessalonians 5:12.

[84] I Timothy 3:4, 5, 12; Titus 3:8, 14.

[85] James Hope Moulton and George Milligan, *The Vocabulary of the Greek Testament* (Grand Rapids, Eerdmans, 1949), p. 551.

[86] *Antiquities*, VII, 380.

[87] Jean Juster, *Les Juifs dans l'empire Romain* (Paris, Paul Geuthner, 1914), I, 442–43.

[88] Emil Schürer, *A History of the Jewish People in the Time of Jesus Christ* (Edinburgh, T. & T. Clark, 1890), Division I, Vol. II, p. 72.

[89] William Sanday and Arthur E. Headlam, *The Epistle to the Romans, International Critical Commentary* (Edinburgh, T. & T. Clark, 1898), p. 418.

[90] J. Armitage Robinson, "Deacon and Deaconess," *Encyclopaedia Biblica* (New York, Macmillan, 1914), p. 1039.

[91] Cf. Lock, *op. cit.*, p. 40.

[92] As H. P. Liddon, *St. Paul's First Epistle to Timothy* (London, Longmans, Green & Co., 1897), p. 34.

PART III

The Status of Women in the Life of the Church During the Second and Third Centuries

Chapter IX

THE AGE OF THE APOSTOLIC FATHERS
AND APOLOGISTS

The period of the Apostolic Fathers and the Apologists roughly carries us throughout the second century. The term *Apostolic Fathers* is regularly used to include literature which was unquestionably not written by Apostolic Fathers, and I wish to include for convenience' sake only several references from writers who were not apologists but who belong to their period. Evidence is not abundant, but certain conclusions are possible from the facts we do have.

THE APOSTOLIC FATHERS

The *Didaché*, which should be dated no earlier than A.D. 90 and no later than A.D. 100,[1] contains instructions for candidates for baptism in the commandments of the Lord as set forth in the Way of Life as opposed to the Way of Death. Part of the instructions concern crediting or discrediting a certain class of traveling missionaries who followed in the wake of the apostles. In Chapter 11, which deals with these prophets, there is no mention or suggestion that women were among their number. Actually the pronouns, relative pronouns, articles, and participles which refer to the prophets are all masculine. It would have been very simple to have written, for instance, *mēdeis auton kai autēn krinetō*, let no one judge him and her, instead of *mēdeis auton krinetō*, let no one judge him.[2] In Chapter 15 where matters concern the appointment of bishops and deacons, all the regulations concern men, and the word *anēr*, which is the word used, refers only to the male sex. Thus we may conclude from the *Didaché* that: (1) if women did have any charismatic ministry it was not of an itinerant nature, (2) the bishops and deacons were men, and (3) the organization of the church did not conclude a definite and official order of deaconesses.

Clement of Rome, whose Epistle to the Corinthians was written A.D. 96, gives us a picture of the early church's concept of the character and work of a woman. One passage concerns household matters:

. . . and the women ye charged to perform all their duties in a blameless and seemly and pure conscience, cherishing their own husbands, as is meet; and yet taught them to keep in the rule of obedience, and to manage the affairs of their household in seemliness, with all discretion.[3]

The other concerns their character:

Let us guide our women toward that which is good: let them show forth their lovely disposition of purity; let them prove their sincere affection of gentleness; let them make manifest the moderation of their tongue through their silence. . . . Let our children be partakers of the instruction which is in Christ.[4]

The writings of Ignatius, whose martyrdom took place during the reign of Trajan (98–117), and probably not before the year 108, furnish more specific information. Two ideas dominate his seven extant letters which were written on his journey of martyrdom from Antioch to Rome. The first concerns the reality of the life and death of the incarnate Son of God in opposition to the prevalent Docetic view. The second is his doctrine of the supremacy of the bishop and implicit obedience to him.[5] However, there is no tinge of sacerdotal language in reference to his ministry nor any idea that the bishop is an autocrat. Obedience is due presbyters and deacons as well, and the purpose of all obedience is to guarantee unity in the church. However, the pertinent point in all this discussion is that in this development of ecclesiastical arrangements deaconesses are significantly absent. Nowhere in his writings are they mentioned.

Widows, however, are mentioned. To Polycarp, Ignatius said: "Let not widows be neglected. After the Lord be thou their protector." [6] To the Smyrnaeans he wrote this word: "I salute the households of my brethren with their wives and children, and the virgins who are called widows." [7] The interpretation of this passage is disputed, for some understand it to indicate that the order of widows was made up of those who were virgins. Others take virgins as a metaphor; that is, these widows were virgins in heart and spirit. Lightfoot argues convincingly for the latter view, and his reasons for rejecting the first view are set forth here.

S. Paul however did not contemplate anything of the kind, for his directions point to widow-hood in the strictest sense, 1 Tim. v. 10. . . . Moreover even at the beginning of the third century Tertullian treats it as a monstrous and unheard-of irregularity that a virgin has been admitted into the order of widows. . . . It seems therefore impossible that at any time when these epistles could have been written, the "viduatus" should have been so largely composed of virgins as to explain the writer's language so interpreted. . . . Moreover with this interpretation we must suppose either that the *chērikon* of Smyrna was *wholly* composed of virgins, or that Ignatius selected out of the order for salutation those only who had never been married. Either supposition would be inexplicable. [8]

The same writer also points out the following:

. . . it was customary to speak of those widows who maintained a chaste widow-hood as "virgins a second time," "virgins in God's sight," and the like; and . . . therefore the expression in *Smyrn.* 13 implies nothing more than that these persons, though widows in common designation and in outward condition, were virgins in heart and spirit. [9]

Thus it seems clear that in Ignatius' time there was a recognized order of widows who were really widows and not virgins, just as was the case in the Pastorals.

About 115 [10] Polycarp, bishop of Smyrna, wrote to the Philippians, and in this epistle is the first extra-Biblical evidence concerning the function of widows. He wrote:

Our widows must be sober-minded as touching the faith of the Lord, making intercession without ceasing for all men [*entugcha-nousas adialeiptōs peri pantōn*], abstaining from all calumny, evil speaking, false witness, love of money, and every evil thing, knowing that they are God's altar [*gunōskousas oti eisi thusiastērion theou*], and that all sacrifices are carefully inspected, and nothing escapeth Him either of their thoughts or intents or any secret things of the heart.[11]

In other words the special work of widows was that of interceding for all men. Since they were called the altar of God they must have been considered in some sense dedicated persons. There is certainly every indication in these words that Polycarp is "referring to the office or order of widows, both from the expressions used . . . and from the position which they occupy immediately before the deacons and priests." [12] It is not evident, however, that there were two classes of widows: those who only received relief and those who in return for their maintenance undertook the special duty of intercession and who were thus enrolled in an order. This passage seems to say that all widows were obliged to render to the church the ministry of intercession, and this seems to have been the regular practice and not an innovation in Polycarp's day.[13]

Other writings generally included under the Apostolic Fathers such as the Epistle of Barnabas and the Shepherd of Hermas contribute nothing of importance to the subject. Thus, in summarizing the evidence of the Apostolic Fathers we may say the following: (1) More frequently than anything else, reference was made to the church's responsibility for the care of its widows. There is no clear evidence for distinguishing between enrolled and unenrolled widows, but all widows ministered to the church by interceding for it. (2) Deaconesses do not appear in any of these writings, and it is only confusion to attempt to equate praying widows with deaconesses. (3) There was no trace of asceticism or preference given to the celibate life.[14] (4) The important work of Christian women in these times was in the home, and concerned proper training of their children.

THE APOLOGISTS

The writings of the Apologists were geared to the days in which they lived. Those days included the display of the omnipotence of Rome, the religious paganism of the nations, the antagonism of Judaism, and the effort of philosophy to discover truth. To meet these four challenges the Apologists wrote, and in their writings certain things concerning the status of women stand out.

The contrast between Christian women and heathen women. The insistent contrast between Christian and pagan women is the most prominent and oft-repeated strain in these writings which is relevant to this book. The higher standards and stricter conduct in relation to Christian women is constantly used as an apologetic for the truth of the Christian message. Justin Martyr (110?–164?) accuses the Greeks of indulging "as a common practice in wicked and insane fornication," and his words clearly imply that it is precisely because of religious beliefs that such practices abound.[15] Tatian (110–180?) also sweepingly condemns the heathen, saying, "You behave yourselves unbecomingly in what relates to woman." [16] The contrast of Christian women is the argument which Athenagoras uses in 176 or 177:

But we are so far from practising promiscuous intercourse, that it is not lawful among us to indulge even a lustful look. "For," saith He, "he that looketh on a woman to lust after her, hath committed adultery in his heart. . . . On behalf of those, then, to whom we apply the names of brothers and sisters, and other designations of relationship, we exercise the greatest care that their bodies should remain undefiled and uncorrupted.[17]

This same contrast of the higher standards of Christianity is described in the *Epistle to Diognetus* (which may be dated about

150). The Christians, says the author, "marry like all other men and they beget children; but they do not cast away their offspring. They have their meals in common, but not their wives." [18] The examples prove the point: Christian women were held in much higher regard than heathen women.

The teaching concerning marriage. The second strain running throughout the writings of the Apologists concerns matters related to marriage. Obviously, all that has just been said concerning standards is relevant to this point too, but in addition, during this period there developed the idea that the primary purpose, if not the only purpose, of marriage was for the procreation of children.[19] However, this was not to the exclusion of any idea of the proper emphasis on love in marriage.[20] Nonetheless, there is a definite beginning of an ascetic strain in Christian teaching during this period. Along with this, as one would naturally expect, came a tendency on the part of some to prefer celibacy; but often celibacy is presented merely as an alternate, and not in preference, to marriage.[21]

NON-CHRISTIAN LITERATURE

In the same period as the Apologists, that is, the second century, there are two important references to women from non-Christian literature. The first is found in the correspondence of Pliny who was sent in 112 by Trajan to be governor of the province of Bithynia in northwest Asia Minor. Pliny was a perfect underling, and when any decision was to be made he wrote to Trajan for advice. Because of Trajan's ban on secret societies, Pliny had to consult the emperor about what to do when he discovered Christian societies spreading in his territory. He wrote as follows: "So I thought it the more necessary to inquire into the real truth of the matter by subjecting to torture two female slaves, who were called deacons [*quae ministrae dicebantur*]; but I found nothing more than a perverse superstition which went beyond all bounds." [22] Of course, the thing that draws our attention to this letter is the reference to the *ministrae.* Since *ministra* is the word which the Vulgate uses to translate *diakonos* in Romans 16:1, it is quite likely that these two female slaves were known in their own Greek-speaking community as *diakonoi*. This is the first reference outside the New Testament to women ministers, but it seems risky to use it to prove the existence of a female diaconate. It would be very difficult to prove that these two women acted in any officially designated capacity in the organization of the church. There is certainly no hint of any official female diaconate. However, the reference does show clearly that virgins, widows, and servants were kept distinct by the early church.

The other reference which concerns widows is in Lucian's account of the wanderings of the philosopher-quack Proteus Peregrinus. In his travels Proteus for a time joined with the Christians and was thrown into prison. The Christians, says Lucian, "left no stone unturned in their endeavour to procure his release. When this proved impossible, they looked after his wants in all other matters with untiring solicitude and devotion. From earliest dawn old women ('widows,' they are called) and orphan children might be seen waiting about the prison-doors; while the officers of the church, by bribing the jailors, were able to spend the night inside with him. Meals were brought in, and they went through their sacred formulas." [23] One might hastily conclude that these widows were the agents of administering the charity, but a closer examination does not lead to such a conclusion. The collocation of "orphan children" with "widows" suggests simply that the two groups who received charity from the church, widows and orphans, gathered at the prison to demonstrate their sympathy by their presence and prayers. In today's parlance they were staging a sympathy demonstration. It is certainly clear that widows were distinguished from the "officers of the church," but it is not clear that these widows performed any regularly assigned, active ministry.

In summarizing the age of the Fathers and the Apologists, we may conclude that during this period the three groups, widows, virgins, and deaconesses, were distinct and separate. Widows were cared for by the church, and in turn they ministered in prayer. Other ministry we cannot see from the evidence. There were no official deaconesses, though women continued to serve the church as they had done since the days of Christ. Celibacy was put forward as an alternate and in some cases a more desirable state than that of marriage, though the definite teaching of preferring celibacy appeared mostly in the literature of the sects of that period.[24] Of the groups of women, widows were undoubtedly the most prominent, and throughout the period there was continuous emphasis on the superiority of the standards and conduct of the lives of Christian women over heathen women.

QUESTIONS

1. Briefly summarize what the Apostolic Fathers said about the place of women.

2. What does the oft-repeated contrast in the writings of the Apologists show about the effect that the Christian message had on the status of women?

NOTES

[1] Burnett Hillman Streeter, *The Primitive Church* (London, Macmillan, 1929), pp. 279–287.

[2] 11:12.

[3] *To the Corinthians,* 1.

[4] *Ibid.,* 21.

[5] *To the Ephesians,* 6; *To the Magnesians,* 6; *To the Trallians,* 2; *To the Smyrnaeans,* 8–9; *To the Philadelphians,* 3.

[6] *To Polycarp,* 4.

[7] *To the Smyrnaeans,* 13.

[8] *The Apostolic Fathers* (London, Macmillan, 1890), II, II, 323.

[9] *Ibid.,* II, I, 399–400.

[10] Cf. Streeter, *op. cit.,* pp. 276–278, for evidence concerning the date.

[11] *To the Philippians,* 4.

[12] Lightfoot, *op. cit.,* II, III, 329.

[13] Lightfoot (*ibid.,* II, II, 322) and Edwin Hatch, "Widows," *A Dictionary of Christian Antiquities* (London, 1908), II, 2034, see two classes of widows. The opposite viewpoint, which is the author's, is supported by C. H. Turner, *The Ministry of Women* (London, SPCK, 1919), p. 89.

[14] Polycarp, *To the Philippians,* 11.

[15] *Discourse to the Greeks,* IV.

[16] *Address to the Greeks,* XXXIII.

[17] *Apology,* XXXII.

[18] Chapter V.

[19] Justin Martyr, *Apology,* I, XXIX and XXXIII.

[20] *Theophilus to Antolycus,* II, XXVIII.

[21] Athenagoras, *Apology,* XXXIII; Eusebius, *Ecclesiastical History,* IV, 23.

[22] Epistle 96.

[23] Lucian, *Death of Peregrinus,* 12.

[24] Cf. Tatian, *Fragments,* III and IX; *Acta Pauli et Theklae,* Sections 5, 6, 11, 12; *Acts of Andrew,* Sections 4–8; Clementine, *Homilies* and *Recognitions.*

Chapter X

THE ALEXANDRIAN FATHERS

The Alexandrian Fathers Clement and Origen have a great deal to say about women in general but very little to say about their p. ce in the public and official life of the church. Clement was born around 150, and although the time and place of his death are unknown, the last mention of him was in a letter written in 211. He lived in an age of transition. "Doctrine was passing from the stage of oral tradition to written definition. . . . Thought was passing from tne immediate circle of the Christian revelation to the whole domain of human experience. . . . Life in its fulness was coming to be apprehended as the object of Christian discipline." [1] In such an age Clement appeared in the role of the Christian philosopher seeking to find the true philosophy in Christ. Gnosticism, of which Alexandria was a hotbed in those days, subordinated religion to philosophy and endeavored to combine evangelical truth with alien beliefs. Clement, though philosophical in his outlook and approach, was careful to insist upon the supreme value of revelation. In everything he expresses the fact that above all else he was a Christian.

In the Gnosticism of his day Clement was confronted with two extreme points of view concerning marriage. The one, championed by Epiphanes the son of Carpocrates, a Gnostic teacher of Alexandria, advocated on a supposedly Scriptural basis free love.[2] The other, supported by followers of Marcion, Tatian the Assyrian, and Julius Cassianus, forbade all marriage and exalted the celibate life.[3] Clement denounced the first as thoroughly un-Christian, and, although he was not without leanings toward an ascetic life, emphatically ruled out the idea of enforced celibacy.

In addition to combating these erroneous teachings in Gnosticism, Clement wrote positively concerning the details of Christian living. Indeed, his own description of the *Paedagogus* is that it describes "what the man who is called a Christian ought to be during the whole of his life." [4] To accomplish this purpose he wrote in minute detail instructions for everything that affects the life of the child of God, including many things concerning relations with women. The instructions were frank, but they were motivated only by a sincere desire to indoctrinate new converts with the high standards of Christianity. "If any justification for his procedure is necessary, it is justified by the consideration that the strength of paganism, from the glamour of which the converts were only just emancipated, lay not so much in its religious conceptions, which could easily be overthrown by arguments, as in the social customs which were an inseparable element in it." [5]

CLEMENT'S VIEWS ON THE STATUS OF WOMEN

Since the writings of Clement are the most lengthy of the early period, it is not surprising to find that he has much to say about the place of women. Often his remarks are tedious, and occasionally it is not easy to reconcile Clement to himself, but nothing he says on this subject is without interest. He considered the subject important to the ordinary believer as well as to the more advanced one, and the many references to women show how practical was his theology and how human was the theologian.

Relation of female to male. In certain respects Clement thought that men and women were equal; namely, in the realm of spiritual things. He said:

Women are therefore to philosophize equally with men, though the males are best at everything, unless they have become effeminate. . . . And how recklessly Euripides writes variously! On one occasion, "For every wife is inferior to her husband, though the most excellent one marry her that is of fair fame." And on another: "For the chaste is her husband's slave. . . ." [6]

It is clear that Clement was opposed to Euripides' idea that the wife is inferior to her husband; indeed, an entire chapter of the *Stromata* is devoted to demonstrating that women as well as men may share in perfection.[7] Especially is this equality in attaining perfection demonstrated in the matter of martyrs:

But as it is noble for a man to die for virtue, and for liberty, and for himself, so also is it for a woman. For this is not peculiar to the nature of males, but to the nature of the good. . . . So we know that both children, and women, and servants have often, against their fathers', and masters', and husbands' will, reached the highest degree of excellence.[8]

Nevertheless, there is also a fundamental difference in nature between male and female which Clement recognized. In speaking of the shame of drunkenness he mentions it quite incidentally but nonetheless definitely when he says, "For nothing disgraceful is proper for man, who is endowed with reason; much less for woman, to whom it brings shame even to reflect of what nature she is."[9] This statement seems to imply inferiority of women, yet in other places Clement makes it clear that the inferiority, or at least the difference in women, is chiefly physical:

We do not say that woman's nature is the same as man's, as she is woman. For undoubtedly it stands to reason that some difference should exist between each of them in virtue of which one is male and the other female. Pregnancy and parturition, accordingly, we say belong to woman, as she is woman, and not as she is a human being. But if there were no difference between man and woman, both would do and suffer the same things. . . . As then there is sameness, as far as respects the soul, she will attain to the same virtue; but as there is difference as respects the peculiar construction of the body, she is destined for childbearing and housekeeping.[10]

Thus, we may say that in the things of the spirit, or in the attaining of maturity in the Christian life, Clement saw no difference

between male and female, but the difference that does exist between the sexes was in the realm of the physical.

The status of women as seen in the marriage relationship. Much
of what Clement said about women falls into this classification. At
times in his writings he seemed to give a decided preference to
celibacy; [11] although, on the other hand, he is just as emphatic in
insisting that marriage is in perfect accord with Christian perfection.[12] In the relationships of marriage Clement disallowed any
lustful designs on women, and he basically had a lofty conception
of a woman's relation to her husband, elevating her to a place of
equality ("a sister in reality" [13]) after she had borne him children.
Procreation of children as the only lawful use of marriage takes
high priority in Clement's thinking.

Clement was quite definite in his ideas about the place of a
woman within the family, for he considered her status to be that of
subordination and the household to be her world. His conception of
subordination and honor for the woman within the family was very
similar to the Jewish idea and not to the Greek or Roman. The detail
of his instructions is extremely interesting; few contemporary preachers would dare express themselves as he did!

Nor are women to be deprived of bodily exercise. But they are not
to be encouraged in wrestling or running, but are to exercise themselves in spinning, and weaving, and superintending the cooking
if necessary. And they are, with their own hand, to fetch from the
store, what we require. And it is no disgrace for them to apply themselves to the mill. Nor is it a reproach to a wife—housekeeper and
helpmeet—to occupy herself in cooking, so that it may be palatable
to her husband. And if she shake up the couch, reach drink to her
husband when thirsty, set food on the table as neatly as possible,
and so give herself exercise tending to sound health, the Instructor
will approve of a woman like this.[14] It is right, then, for men to re-
pose confidence in their wives, and commit the charge of the household to them as they are given to be their helpers in this. . . . For
a most beautiful thing is a thrifty wife, who clothes both herself and
her husband with fair array of her own working.[15]

Evidently Clement would have subscribed to the maxim that a woman's work is never done, for he says (in all seriousness):

For those who have the sleepless Word dwelling in them ought not to sleep the livelong night, but they ought to rise by night . . . and one devote himself to literature, another being his art, the women handle the distaff, and all of us should, so to speak, fight against sleep.[16]

In all of these matters it is very important to note that Clement insisted that his teaching followed that of the apostles. He cites such passages from the New Testament as I Corinthians 7 concerning the acceptability of celibacy, and Ephesians 5 and Colossians 3 concerning the headship of the husband and the subordination of the wife.[17] Thus he did not believe that he was in any wise introducing something new but simply reiterating the teaching of the apostles.

The status of women in church relationships. Clement has very little to say that would throw any light on the official status women had in his day in the organized church. Woman's service for Christ was primarily in the home. There is no evidence of an order of widows, though of course the silence does not prove that an order did not exist. Women, however, are instructed to be veiled when they go to church, "since it is becoming for her to pray veiled." [18] If she took any part in the public worship other than prayer Clement does not mention it. However, Clement did believe that Paul's reference to leading about "a sister, a wife" [19] was not a reference to the wives of the apostles but to ministering women who accompanied the apostles in their ministry. He refers to these ministering women (*diakonōn gunaikōn*), whom as fellow ministers (*sundiakonoi*) the apostles took with them, "not as wives, but as sisters" [20] in order that they might give themselves without distraction to the ministry of the Word. But Clement did not say or even allude to the possibility that in his own day such was being done by individuals or by a class of women who might be considered as an order of deaconesses. Other references to any official status of women in the church are not to be found in Clement's writings, and one would conclude that he considered that their place, as the apostles had taught before him, was primarily in the home.

In summarizing Clement's views on the status of women, one may say that in the realm of the spirit, and as far as spiritual responsibilities were concerned, he considered that there was no difference between male and female. The basic difference was in the sphere of the physical. He seemed to feel that this was an inferior position to that of man's; it certainly involved different responsibilities. He clearly reasserted the Pauline principle of the headship of the husband in the home. As in all the teaching of the early church, women were protected from all immorality and immodesty in Clement's ethic. The very fact that he went into so much detail in guiding women in the conduct of their faith bespeaks a more exacting moral standard than that which existed in heathen society of his day. Even in the domestic duties assigned to women there is nothing of the ancient Greek idea of confinement but much more of the Jewish conception that the home with its duties and responsibilities under the headship of the husband is the place of honor which God has designated for the woman. If one's idea of the advance and liberation of women must exclude the idea of "helpmeet" with its concept of subordination, then one will say that Clement taught a very narrow concept. But one thing is absolutely certain—Clement himself did not think such ideas were a reversion in any sense, for all the principles he set forth are part of true Christian Gnosticism, and one could have no higher goal in life than to be a true Gnostic. Unfortunately, we have to be content with the relative silence concerning the work of women in the organization of the church. One can only suggest that evidently there had been little change from the ministry of women in the church of New Testament days.

ORIGEN'S VIEWS ON THE STATUS OF WOMEN

Origen, who succeeded Clement as head of the Catechetical School in Alexandria, was born in that city in 185, became head of the school at the age of eighteen, spent the next twelve years in extreme self-denial, increasing wisdom, and brilliant teaching, and finally died after persecution by both ecclesiastical and secular authorities in 253 at Tyre. Though his writings were numerous, what has been lost is far more than what has been preserved, and in them there is only a relatively small amount of material which reflects his opinion concerning the status of women.

In relation to Clement's, Origen's contribution to this subject is much less. Nevertheless he does make clear a few ideas concerning women. He assigns an inferior position to the female sex,[21] although he does not connect it with his view of the fall of man.[22] Neither does he elaborate as to what this subordination means. Clearer, however, is the more meritorious position assigned to the life of virginity and celibacy in contrast to the married state, for he declared, "But God has allowed us to marry, because all are not fit for the higher, that is, the perfectly pure life." [23] Furthermore, commenting on Romans 16:1–2, he says, "This passage . . . shows that women also were set in the ministry of the Church; in which office Phoebe was placed in the Church which is in Cenchreae." [24] Evidently he believed that Phoebe occupied an official position, but he gives no indication that there was anything like an order of deaconesses in his own day. Since this is all that he said relevant to the subject, it is clear that his contribution was small and indecisive.

QUESTIONS

1. Do the writings of Clement of Alexandria reveal any new ideas about the place of women or simply reiterate what the New Testament says?

2. Do you think Clement had any un-Scriptural ideas about the place of women?

NOTES

[1] Brooke Foss Westcott, "Clement of Alexandria," *A Dictionary of Christian Biography* (London, John Murray, 1877), I, 560.

[2] *Stromata*, III, Chaps. II and IV.

[3] *Ibid.*, III, Chaps. III and V. Cf. Henry Melvill Gwatkin, *Early Church History* (London, Macmillan, 1927), II, 67–68.

[4] *Paedagogus*, II, I.

[5] John Patrick, *Clement of Alexandria* (Edinburgh, W. Blackwood & Sons, 1914), p. 13.

[6] *Stromata*, IV, VIII.

[7] IV, XIX.

[8] *Stromata*, IV, VIII. For a good summary of women martyrs in the early church, cf. Leopold Zscharnack, *Der Dienst der Frau in den ersten Jahrhunderten der christlichen Kirche* (Göttingen, Vandenhoeck & Ruprecht, 1902), pp. 27–37.

[9] *Paedagogus*, II, II.

[10] *Stromata*, IV, VIII.

[11] *Ibid.*, III, I; VI, XII.

[12] *Ibid.*, VII, XII.

[13] *Ibid.*, VI, XII.

[14] *Paedagogus*, III, X.

[15] *Ibid.*, III, XI.

[16] *Ibid.*, II, IX.

[17] *Stromata*, III, XII; VII, XI; IV, VIII.

[18] *Paedagogus*, III, XI.

[19] I Corinthians 9:5.

[20] *Stromata*, III, VI.

[21] *Commentary on Matthew*, XIV, 16.

[22] Norman Powell Williams, *The Ideas of the Fall and of Original Sin* (London, Longmans, Green & Co., 1927), p. 225.

[23] *Against Celsus*, VIII, LV. Cf. *ibid.*, VII, XLVIII; I, XXVI; *Commentary on Matthew*, XIV, 25.

[24] *Commentary on Romans*, X, 17.

Chapter XI

THE AFRICAN FATHERS

From our consideration of the Alexandrian Fathers we turn now to those of a region not remote geographically from Egypt (though theologically so), the Roman proconsular province of Africa, generally called North Africa. Nothing is known about the founding or early history of the church in this region, though the first two church fathers known to us from the churches of North Africa are the two we want to consider in this chapter—Tertullian and Cyprian.

TERTULLIAN'S LIFE AND TIMES

Quintus Septimius Florens Tertullianus was born about 160, a native of Carthage, which was at that time a wealthy, enterprising city with a flourishing church which was constantly being tempted to make her Christianity as fashionable as Carthage was. Tertullian was trained as an advocate, in the course of which training he spent some time in Rome and Athens. He was converted sometime between 192 and 195, and according to his own testimony it was a conversion from all the sins of heathenism. About 201 he left the church and embraced the beliefs of Montanism, writing a number of his extant works after this. He died about 230.

It is necessary to know something of the background of the man and his times in order to understand his writings. Because he was a lawyer, his writings are cast in a rhetorical and argumentative style. When he was converted he cast away all his heathen past, so that there is not one false ring in his writings. To him beliefs were no barren dogmas or matters for mere discussion; hence his works are permeated with intense personal fervor. He lacked patience and breadth of understanding in his zeal for the truth, and yet he himself was painfully aware of his own shortcomings.[1] He was a rigorist through and through, and it is no wonder that Montanism held attractions for such a man.

Because Montanism did have such a great influence in the life and writings of Tertullian, we must consider some of the teachings of that sect. In the second century Gnosticism and Montanism were the two major deviations from catholic teaching. The Gnostics may be said to have leaned too much to the intellectual side of Christianity and the Montanists to what might be called the inspirational side. However, unlike the Gnostics, the Montanists did not for the most part deviate far from the foundations of truth. To understand fully Montanism one must first trace its antecedents. In apostolic days, of course, the prophet was a recognized figure in church life. What he spoke through the Holy Spirit was considered binding,[2] and he is placed second only to the apostle in the listing of gifts to the church.[3] According to the *Didaché* the prophet still occupied at the end of the first century a place of honor. However, it is not difficult to see how tension would arise between the authority of the prophet and that of the leaders of the local congregation. The *Didaché* gave instructions which would maintain a balance between these two persons, but shortly thereafter Ignatius by stressing the supremacy of the single bishop practically excluded the proper exercise of prophecy. It is not difficult to see how such tension could easily develop into a schism, which is exactly what did happen in Montanism, the chief manifestation of prophetism in the post-apostolic age.

It was in the highlands of Phrygia that this new religious activity appeared about 156. Montanus himself was not really a great man, but he had the ability to attract minds superior to his own. Indeed, "the sect would have made but a small ripple on the surface of Christendom, if the wayward genius of Tertullian had not lent energy to its propaganda." [4] Montanus taught that just as the dispensation of the Father had given place to the dispensation of the Son at the Incarnation, so the dispensation of the Son had given place to the dispensation of the Spirit. Christ's promise of the coming of the Paraclete had been fulfilled, and Montanus was the Paraclete's mouthpiece. All of this was the prelude to the second advent of Christ who would establish the New Jerusalem in Phrygia. Two of Montanus' followers, and the most notable, were women, Priscilla and Maximilla. They were not only companions of their leader but also sharers in the gift of prophecy.[5]

What appealed to Tertullian in Montanism was its insistence on a high standard of conduct for Christians. Since the world was doomed and since the end was near, Christians should in a very literal sense leave the world by living more austere and holy lives. This is what appealed to Tertullian's stern and uncompromising nature. Such a man who broke so completely with heathenism when he was converted would naturally welcome any movement that would purify conditions in the church and would give it his hearty support in enforcing its standards. Cruttwell summarizes the situation well in these words:

The standard of holiness had sunk very low. Worldliness was rampant among those who should have set an example of self-denial. The effeminate luxury of the priesthood excited his [Tertullian's] daily scorn: the love of dress had made the very Virgins of the Church vie with their heathen sisters in each art that could captivate the eye of man. Even the veil, that immemorial badge of maiden modesty, was discarded. Christian men and women frequented the public shows, these vile nurseries of profligacy and cruelty. It seemed as if the Church had striven to quench the Spirit, and the Spirit, affronted, had deserted the Church.[6]

Small wonder that such a movement in such surroundings would appeal to such a man.

TERTULLIAN'S VIEWS ON THE STATUS OF WOMEN

Relation of the sexes. Cadoux called Tertullian a "woman-hater"[7] because he maintained that there was a fundamental distinction between the sexes, which was plainly the difference of the superiority of the male and the inferiority of the female. In dealing

with the question of the veiling of virgins, Tertullian, arguing from
the greater to the lesser, stated that if certain liberties were not
allowed male virgins (eunuchs) they certainly were not to be
allowed female virgins.[8] In the same place he clearly says that
females are "subjected . . . throughout to men." Moreover, not only
did Tertullian hold these views but he linked this inferior position
of women to the Fall. Mincing no words, he said:

If there dwelt upon earth a faith as great as is the reward of faith
which is expected in the heavens, no one of you at all, best beloved
sisters, from the time that she had first "known the Lord," and
learned concerning her own (that is, woman's) condition, would
have desired too gladsome (not to say too ostentatious) a style of
dress; so as not rather to go about in humble garb, and rather to
affect meanness of appearance, walking about as Eve mourning and
repentant, in order that by every garb of penitence she might the
more fully expiate that which she derives from Eve,—the ignominy,
I mean, of the first sin, and the odium of human perdition. "In pains
and in anxieties dost thou bear, woman; and toward thine husband
thy inclination, and he lords it over thee." And do you not know
that you are each an Eve? The sentence of God on this sex of yours
lives in this age: the guilt must of necessity live too. *You* are the
devil's gateway: *you* are the unsealer of that tree: *you* are the first
deserter of the divine law: *you* are she who persuaded him whom
the devil was not valiant enough to attack. *You* destroyed so easily
God's image, man. On account of *your* desert—that is, death—even
the Son of God had to die.[9]

Thus the subjection of woman to man is clearly related to her part
in the original sin.

Marriage and celibacy. The contrast, which was so evident in
the Apologists, between the high standards of Christianity and
those of the heathen in relation to women is also found in the writings of Tertullian. In his *Apology* he charged the heathen with
illicit intercourse, incest, exposure of children, and lustful indul-
gence in general. Of the Christian, by contrast, he said:

A persevering and steadfast chastity has protected us from anything like this: keeping as we do from adulteries and all post-matrimonial unfaithfulness, we are not exposed to incestuous mishaps. . . . If you would but take notice that such sins as I have mentioned prevail among you, that would lead you to see that they have no existence among Christians.[10]

However, there is also found in Tertullian the continuance of the developing strain of asceticism. The idea of the meritoriousness of the celibate life is dominant in his writings,[11] and yet Christian marriage did not lack esteem in his estimation.[12] But in giving the preference to celibacy, Tertullian considered himself to be following the teaching of the apostles,[13] and he was motivated by the nearness of the Lord's coming.[14] Should a woman marry, Tertullian clearly taught that she was to submit herself to her husband as to her lord and that her duties should be to "busy your hands with spinning; keep your feet at home; and you will 'please' better than by arraying yourselves in gold." [15] He also taught that the sphere of the woman was the home of which her husband was the head.

Virgins. The question which naturally follows from this preference to celibacy is, Is there any evidence of the existence of an order of virgins in Tertullian's time? At the beginning of the second century Polycarp had admonished virgins to make their vows known only to the bishop. A hundred years later Tertullian was battling to maintain this private character of dedicating one's life to virginity, and he was battling against a group of virgins who had appeared unveiled in the church. Since girls under the age of betrothal wore no veils, certain of the dedicated virgins were maintaining that since they were living in a continuation of this age of innocency they should be allowed to appear also unveiled. Tertullian's answer to this was as follows:

It is not permitted to a *woman* to speak in the church; but neither is it permitted her to teach, nor to baptize, nor to offer, nor to claim to herself a lot in any manly function, not to say sacerdotal office. Let us inquire whether any of these be lawful to a *virgin*. If it is *not* lawful to a *virgin,* but she is subjected on the selfsame terms as a *woman,* whence will this one thing be lawful to *her* which is not lawful to any and every *female?* Is the reason why it is granted her to dispense with the veil, that she may be notable and marked as she enters the church? that she may display the honor of sanctity in the liberty of her head? More worthy distinction could have been conferred on her by according her some prerogative of manly rank or office! [16]

The rest of Tertullian's argument does not concern us, for certain points have been clearly made. They are: (1) in the fact that certain churches did have the custom of allowing its virgins to appear unveiled in the congregation is evidence of the beginnings of the process which finally separated a virgin from her fellow Christians. Probably Tertullian's stand against this retarded the development of orders of virgins in the West. (2) No special functions, and certainly no liturgical functions, were allowed virgins any more than other women. (3) There is indication that the church undertook the maintenance of virgins at least in Montanist groups.[17] How this can be reconciled with the insistence on the private character of the virgin's vows is a mystery.

Widows. We have already seen that during the first and second century the widow was the prominent figure in the church. Widows were enrolled and expected to intercede for the church. Thus they came to be regarded in a certain sense as dedicated persons; consequently, it is not surprising to discover that in Tertullian's time widows had a special place assigned to them in the church. Tertullian speaks of it almost in passing in connection with the matter of a repentant sinner:

Why, do you yourself, when introducing into the church, for the purpose of melting the brotherhood by his prayers, the repentant adulterer, lead into the midst and prostrate him, all in haircloth and ashes, a compound of disgrace and horror, before the widows, before the elders, suing for the tears of all, licking the footprints of all, clasping the knees of all? [18]

Widows were evidently a distinguishable group in the congregation, and one which was accorded a certain honor.

However, specific regulations governed admittance into the catalogue of widows. The minimum age was sixty years; widows were to be married once and only once; and they were to be mothers. All of this is seen as Tertullian expostulates:

I know plainly, that in a certain place a virgin of less than twenty years of age has been placed in the order of *widows!* whereas if the bishop had been bound to accord her any relief, he might, of course, have done it in some other way without detriment to the respect due to discipline; that such a miracle, not to say a monster, should not be pointed at in the church, a *virgin-widow!* the more portentous indeed, that not even as a *widow* did she veil her head; denying herself either way; both as *virgin*, in that she is counted a *widow*, and as *widow*, in that she is styled a *virgin*. But the authority which licenses her sitting in that seat *uncovered* is the same which allows her to sit here as a *virgin; a* seat to which (besides the "sixty years") not merely "single-husbanded" women—that is, *married women*—are at length elected, but "mothers" to boot, yes, and "educators of children"; in order, forsooth, that their experimental training in all the affections may, on the one hand, have rendered them capable of readily aiding all others with counsel and comfort, and that, on the other, they may nonetheless have travelled down the whole course of probation whereby a *female* can be tested. So true is it, that on the ground of her position, nothing in the way of public honor is permitted to a *virgin*.[19]

Thus specific requirements were laid down for the order of widows who were a distinct group in the church and the women's group that took prominence over all others, including virgins.

The public ministry of women. We have already seen that Tertullian believed that the primary ministry of a woman is in the home. That is further emphasized by his answer to the question, When should a woman be allowed to appear in public?

You, however [in contrast to Gentile women who go to the temple and public shows], have no cause of appearing in public, except such as is serious. Either some brother who is sick is visited, or else the sacrifice is offered, or else the word of God is dispensed.[20]

However, he did not mean that a woman could dispense the word of God in the public assembly, because he also wrote concerning a false woman teacher: "And so that most monstrous creature, who had no right to teach even sound doctrine [as being a woman], knew full well how to kill the little fishes, by taking them away from the water." [21] Speaking further of women who belonged to heretical sects, he said: "The very women of these heretics, how wanton they are! For they are bold enough to teach, to dispute, to enact exorcisms, to undertake curses—it may be even to baptize." [22] And finally, speaking of the story of Paul and Thekla, he based his proof that it was a forgery on the fact that it was contrary to Paul's teaching: "For how credible would it seem that he who has not permitted a *woman* even to *learn* with over-boldness, should give a *female* the power of *teaching* and of *baptizing!* 'Let them be silent,' he says, 'and at home consult their own husbands.' " [23]

When Tertullian became a Montanist his views concerning women were more carefully defined and detailed. The same strictness regarding their public ministry as he held in pre-Montanist days carried over: "It is not permitted to a *woman* to speak in the church; but neither is it permitted her to teach, nor to baptize, nor to offer, nor to claim to herself a lot in any manly function, not to say sacerdotal office." [24] However, it is clear that under certain circumstances he approved of women receiving revelations. The following passage demonstrating this was written concerning a Montanist assembly:

We have now amongst us a sister whose lot it has been to be favored with sundry gifts of revelation, which she experiences in the Spirit by ecstatic vision amidst the sacred rites of the Lord's day in the church: she converses with angels, and sometimes even with the Lord; she both sees and hears mysterious communications. Some men's hearts she understands, and to them who are in need she distributes remedies. Whether it be in the reading of the Scriptures, or in the chanting of psalms, or in the preaching of sermons, or in the offering up of prayers, in all these religious services matter and opportunity are afforded to her of seeing visions. . . . After the people are dismissed at the conclusion of the sacred services, she is in the regular habit of reporting to us whatever things she may have seen in a vision (for all her communications are examined with the most scrupulous care, in order that their truth may be proved).[25]

In public ministry, then, Tertullian granted women a little more freedom than those leaders of the church who went before him. But it is very little more, and it is definitely related to the Montanist sect. He still considered the home to be a woman's sphere, but he said less about that and much more about virgins and widows than his predecessors. All of this seems to indicate that in his day Christian women were taking a much larger place in public life.

CYPRIAN'S LIFE AND TIMES

From the days of Tertullian to those of Augustine only the name of Cyprian is outstanding in the African church. Little is known of his early life, but he was evidently a man of means, education, a master of rhetoric, and probably an advocate. The place and date of his birth are unknown, although he was converted in 246 in middle life, which means he was probably born about the turn of the century. Though he lived only eleven years after his conversion, he rose rapidly in position and influence in the church. Less than three years after his baptism he was made bishop of Carthage, and he served the church until he was beheaded under the persecution of Valerian in 257.[26]

During his times Cyprian was forced to deal with several controversial problems in the church. Just after his selection as bishop he was faced with the matter of holy women and holy men living together, and during his ministry there were controversies over those who lapsed in their faith because of the Decian persecution and over the rebaptism of heretics and schismatics. In all of Cyprian's writings it is evident that Tertullian is his master both in that he imitated Tertullian's style and in that his writings lack the depth of Tertullian's. And yet in the handling of the difficult problems which arose during his time, Cyprian always displays "the gentleness of the Christian, as well as the prudence of the man of the world, and the sagacious judgment of the ruler." [27]

CYPRIAN'S VIEWS ON THE STATUS OF WOMEN

The public ministry of women. Cyprian reaffirms the apostolic dictum that there is neither male nor female in Christ Jesus by saying, "Whence it appeared that the mercy of Christ, and the heavenly grace that would subsequently follow, was equally divided among all; without difference of sex, without distinction of years, without accepting of persons, upon all the people of God the gift of spiritual grace was shed." [28] Of the unity and equality of the sexes in spiritual bonds there was no question. However, women were not to speak in the church, for in the collection of divine precepts known as *Testimonies Against the Jews* Cyprian stated clearly "that a woman ought to be silent in the church." As support he cited I Corinthians 14:34–35 and I Timothy 2:11–14.[29] Thus his idea of equality does not include spiritual activity.

Widows. Little was said about widows except that the church was noted for "so many praiseworthy widows." [30] Cyprian says much more about virgins, but it must not be assumed that widows were the less prominent group. Virgins were the troublesome group, and most of what is said about them is the result of abuse and wrong conduct on their part which called forth strenuous and verbose writing by the bishop of that church. We also know that in the church at Rome at the same time (about A.D. 250) there were more than 1,500 widows on the roll to be supported by the church.[31] Thus the relative amount of space Cyprian devotes to widows should not be assumed to mean that they had become less prominent; rather we conclude that the picture had not changed since the days of Tertullian and that widows still occupied an honored place as a recognized order in the church.

Virgins. Cyprian has much to say about virgins, whom he held in very high esteem [32] and who furnished him with one of the first problems he had as bishop. In the enthusiasm of the first flush of the Christian experience, and also probably out of the very practical necessity of finding houses for converted girls who had been disowned by their parents, virgins lived together with men in the same houses and often in the same rooms. Although in most instances there was nothing immoral about the relationship, it did become scandalous, and Cyprian had to deal with it by laying down certain requirements and tests for the admission or exclusion of such from the fellowship of the church.[33] A second problem which confronted Cyprian concerned the dress of virgins. He devoted an entire treatise to this matter—many of the phrases of which are exactly Tertullian's —in an attempt to curb this tendency on the part of virgins to be too much like other women in their dress. His argument is based on the premise that virginity means holiness in every respect, and he appeals to many Scriptures to prove it.[34]

The details and minutiae of Cyprian's answers to these problems do not concern us; the question which does concern us is, Can we see a beginning of an order of virgins in the church of Cyprian's day? I personally feel that we cannot. Those who argue for the existence of a rudimentary order cite two facts: [35] (1) Cyprian admonished older virgins to teach younger ones,[36] and (2) he treated virgins with more deference than Tertullian did, as if to imply that they had become a recognized order in the church.[37] But to me neither of these arguments seems convincing. The first has no more meaning than the same instruction in Titus 2 where certainly no order of virgins is in view. The second, which amounts to a difference in style of writing, is too easily accounted for by the difference in writers. An order of virgins—no; the trends which eventually led to an order—yes. The increasing prominence given to virgins, the matters related to their being distinguished in the congregation by their plain dress, and the ever-present tendency to prefer the celibate life are the trends. But trends are one thing, and a clear organization is quite another.

Thus during this period in the African church, widows were still the prominent group, though virgins were gaining more mention and recognition; the trend toward the celibate life continued, no official ministry was assigned to women, and deaconesses did not appear at all in the writings of the period.

QUESTIONS

1. What was Montanism, and how did it influence the mind of Tertullian?

2. What did Tertullian think should be done about a woman who was in the habit of receiving revelations from God during church services?

3. What place did virgins begin to occupy by Cyprian's time?

NOTES

[1] *De Pudicitia*, 1.
[2] Cf. Acts 11:27–30.
[3] I Corinthians 12:28; Ephesians 4:11.
[4] R. A. Knox, *Enthusiasm* (New York, Oxford University Press, 1950), p. 25.
[5] Eusebius, *Ecclesiastical History*, IV, 27; V, 16–18.
[6] Thomas Charles Cruttwell, *A Literary History of Early Christianity* (London, 1893), II, 557.
[7] Cecil John Cadoux, *The Early Church and the World* (Edinburgh, T. & T. Clark, 1925), p. 443.
[8] *De Virginibus Velandis*, 10.
[9] *De Cultu Feminarum*, I, 1.
[10] *Apology*, 9.
[11] *Ad Uxorem*, I, 3; *Adversus Marcion*, V, 15; *De Monogamia*, 3.
[12] *Ad Uxorem*, II, 8.
[13] *Ibid.*, I, 3.
[14] *De Monogamia*, 3, 16; *Ad Uxorem*, I, 5.
[15] *De Cultu Feminarum*, II, 13.
[16] *De Virginibus Velandis*, 4.
[17] *Ibid.*, 14.
[18] *De Pudicitia*, 13.
[19] *De Virginibus Velandis*, 9; cf. *Ad Uxorem*, I, 7.
[20] *De Cultu Feminarum*, II, 11. This was written before Tertullian embraced Montanism.
[21] *De Baptismo*, 1.
[22] *De Praescriptione Haereticorum*, 41.
[23] *De Baptismo*, 17.
[24] *De Virginibus Velandis*, 9.
[25] *De Anima*, 9.
[26] Cf. Pontius, *Life and Passion of Cyprian, Bishop and Martyr*.
[27] Cruttwell, *op. cit.*, II, 600.
[28] Epistle 75 (69 in Oxford ed.), 14.
[29] Book III, Number 46.
[30] Epistle 68 (66 in Oxford ed.), 7.
[31] Eusebius, *Ecclesiastical History*, VI, 43.
[32] Epistle 54 (59 in Oxford ed.), 13; Epistle 51 (55 in Oxford ed.), 20; *On the Dress of Virgins*, 3.

[33] Epistle 61 (4 in Oxford ed.), 1–4. Cf. also John Alfred Faulkner, *Cyprian: The Churchman* (Cincinnati, 1906), pp. 52–53.

[34] No less than 35 Scriptures are cited or alluded to in the treatise *On the Dress of Virgins*.

[35] As Edward White Benson, *Cyprian: His Life, His Times, His Work* (London, Macmillan, 1897), p. 52.

[36] *On the Dress of Virgins*, 21.

[37] *Ibid.*, 3, "I exhort with affection rather than with power. . . ."

Chapter XII

THE THIRD CENTURY CHURCH ORDERS

It would seem logical to the modern mind that the early church would have desired to codify regulations which existed in the days of the apostles for the conduct of Christian assemblies. After all, the apostles themselves had dealt with such matters, as witnessed by the attention given in their writings to such details as seating people in church, visiting the sick, regular meetings of the church, and the necessity of work.[1] However, as the first leaders passed away it was not the codifying of regulations for the conduct of the assemblies which was first felt to be necessary, but rather the writing down of the message of Christianity together with the facts, incidents, and stories surrounding the life of its Founder.

However, in the Ante-Nicene period there are four extant documents which may be classified as Church Orders. Except for the *Didaché* they all belong to the third century and are known as *The Apostolic Tradition* of Hippolytus, the *Apostolic Church Order*, and the *Didascalia*. *The Testament of the Lord*, another Church Order with an apocryphal setting making considerable use of the *Apostolic Tradition*, is probably as late as the fifth century,[2] and the *Apostolic Constitutions* which embody the *Didascalia* in Books I–VI, the *Didaché* in Book VII, and the *Apostolic Tradition* in Book VIII "can now with some confidence be assigned to a date about A.D. 375 and to the region of Antioch."[3]

In using these writings two factors must be kept in mind. First, they were not regarded as widely authoritative. As another says:

. . . it was the instinctive feeling of the Church that traditions of this kind, fettering the free development of Church legislation on things indifferent, were of minor importance, if not harmful. . . . They compare unfavourably not only with the canonical books but with genuine Sub-Apostolic literature.[4]

Second, although they were not considered authoritative, they do furnish a picture of church practice in that early period. Nevertheless:

. . . not one of those Church-Orders which we have to handle is strictly speaking a unit: they all include different historic strata side by side, whether by way of simple accretion by means of additions or interpolations, or in virtue of the working-up of earlier historical units into some fresh organic synthesis. . . .[5]

THE APOSTOLIC TRADITION

This writing, which is best dated in the year 215, has been decisively demonstrated to be the work of the anti-pope and martyr Hippolytus.[6] It was written in the midst of controversy, for both the prologue and epilogue declare in substance that where Christian life is ordered after the pattern of this manual there and only there will be found an authentic assembly and true doctrine. That it was a work of controversy does not mean it was subject to bias and inaccuracies. Indeed, the circumstances surrounding its writing argue for the opposite conclusion. Another puts it this way:

He is openly attacking what he considers the innovating tendencies of those with whom he is at loggerheads on other grounds by making a public appeal to the past. In the circumstances it is of the very essence of his case that he should, for the most part at least, be really doing what he says he is doing, setting down genuine old Roman customs and rules of which the memory of Roman Christians then "went not back to the contrary." [7]

Thus Hippolytus was not composing a set of original rules but was setting down existing customs, and "we may safely take it that in outline and essentials the rites and customs to which the *Apostolic*

Tradition bears witness were those practised in the Roman Church in his own day, and in his own youth *c.* A.D. 180." [8] Further, it probably represented generally the practice of the whole church in that period, for although it did not have much influence in the Roman Church it does represent its customs, and we know from the use made of it in the *Apostolic Constitutions* that it was circulated and followed in Syria. Gregory Dix sums up the value of this work as follows:

We can watch Hippolytus at work on his material, adapting and supplementing a little here and there with his own comments, perhaps in one or two cases misunderstanding the origin and intention of the practices already ancient which he describes. But making all due allowance for these cases, there remains a much larger part of the contents, some of it supported by allusions in other writers, of which we can safely say that his material comes to him rather than from him. It represents the mind and practice not of St. Hippolytus only but of the whole Catholic Church of the second century. As such it is of outstanding importance. [9]

Concerning widows this manual states three important facts. First, widows were not ordained as were bishops, presbyters, and deacons. The reason for this is specifically stated—"because she does not offer the oblation nor has she a liturgical ministry." [10] Second, widows who had been tested for a time were allowed to be enrolled on the church's lists. [11] This evidently means that there were two groups of widows or at least that there were widows and probationers. Third, the ministry of widows, besides being stated negatively as not being liturgical, is stated positively as being that of prayer. Further, they were to be ministered to in material things by members of the congregation. [12]

Of virgins it is only stated that "the Virgin is not appointed but voluntarily separated and named. A Virgin does not have an imposition of hands, for personal choice alone is that which makes a virgin." [13] This is quite in line with earlier evidence which showed that widows assumed a far more prominent place than virgins, who did not become anything approaching an order until near the end of the Ante-Nicene period.

In the assembly itself the women were to "stand . . . by themselves apart from the men, both the baptised women and the women catechumens." [14] In addition, women were to be veiled,[15] but this is not connected in any way with the Fall of man or with any idea of inferiority of the female sex.

One further regulation is of interest. Hippolytus says: "If a man's concubine be a slave, let her hear the word on condition that she have reared her children, and if she consorts with him alone. But if not let her be rejected." [16] The practice of slavery with all its abuses continually plagued the church with problems. Among them was the problem of the unions between slaves and freemen. Roman law did not recognize any union with a slave as full marriage (*matrimonium*) but only as a concubinage (*contubernium*). Even if such a union were permanent, it was never recognized as marriage before the law. The church, therefore, according to this regulation in the *Apostolic Tradition*, took steps to elevate the status of slave women by recognizing as full Christian marriage a slave's concubinage provided she reared the children and consorted with one man only. Such a girl was not only considered married but was allowed into full fellowship of the church. In effect the church was creating its own ecclesiastical law of marriage in contrast to the existing civil law, and in doing so elevated the status of a certain group of women.

Finally, we note the absence of any mention of deaconesses in this work. Even in the canons concerning baptism, and although anointings are mentioned, nothing is said of the ministration of women in these anointings even when women are the ones being baptized.

THE APOSTOLIC CHURCH ORDER

Harnack places the date of the final form of this work around the year 300, but insists that the sources which the editor used are as early as the year 200. Evidently the editing, measured quantitatively, has been small, and everything points to Egypt as the place where it was done, although Asia Minor was probably the original area of the sources.[17] In spite of the fact that we have before us very early sources, the document could hardly be called a monument in the early church or a document which arose from one of the chief churches.

The principal contribution of this document to the subject under discussion concerns widows. Section 21 says:

Three widows shall be appointed, two to persevere in prayer for all those who are in temptation, and for the reception of revelations where such are necessary, but one to assist the women visited with sicknesses, she must be ready for service [*eudiakonos*], discreet, communicating what is necessary to the presbyters, not avaricious, not given to much love of wine, so that she may be sober and capable of performing the night services [*hupēresias*], and other loving service if she will; for these are the chief good treasures of the Lord.

Bartlet has pointed out that this Church Order belongs to a region where the church was largely in a missionary stage. If this is true then

the work becomes the more interesting in this light, as directing our attention to the things felt to be most essential . . . which determined first the original forms and then the changes made in them.[18]

However, the changes, as Harnack shows, in the original forms were not in the list of those who make up the organization of the church but only in the numbers within each group, not in the number of groups; thus, it becomes extremely significant that widows appear in a list which includes bishops, presbyters, readers, and deacons. The ministry of women was evidently felt to be a real need in a newly organized assembly. This would, however, be without any special significance if these widows were simply designated to be intercessors for the congregation, for this function of widows appeared early and often in the literature of the Ante-Nicene period. That widows should be nurses of sick women is not especially surprising, but what is new is, first, that widows are expected to receive revelations, and, second, that there is a division of responsibility among them, two being appointed for intercession, and one to nursing. The idea that intercessory widows would receive revelations surely reflects Montanist influence, and although these revelations were "in relation to the necessities of the members of the congregation," yet it is evident that "a *charisma* of the widows is of course presupposed." [19]

It is this division of labor among the widows which is most interesting, especially in the light of another passage which definitely restricts the public ministry of women and denies to them anything like a formal diaconate.[20] Yet the extraordinary thing is that in spite of these limitations the nursing widow is assigned responsibilities which correspond to those later assigned to deaconesses. Evidently the ministry of women and their official status was in a state of flux or perhaps in controversy in the period when the Order was written, but it appears that we are standing in the vestibule of an organization which will include deaconesses in the official sense.

THE SYRIAN DIDASCALIA

The third Church Order which belongs to the period under discussion is the so-called *Didascalia*. Connolly, who has written the most comprehensive English work on the subject, places its date of writing in the first part of the third century before the Decian persecution,[21] and he locates the place of composition as being between Antioch and Edessa. It is the most important of the sources of this study, for as no other ancient Christian writing, it gives detailed information concerning the life of the ancient Christian community. It is primarily concerned with Christian living as a whole, and it relates every institutional element to that life in a vital way; thus, this document stands alone in its class as a faithful portrayal of church life in the third century.

Of woman's place in the official life of the church much is said. However, nothing is said at all about a preference for the celibate life or about an order of virgins. This is in marked contrast with Western thought as witnessed in the Church Order of Hippolytus and in the writings of Tertullian and Cyprian. Of widows, however, much is said.

Widows were divided into two classes—those who were enrolled in an order and those who were not. Evidently the only qualification for being enrolled was age, and that was ten years younger than laid down in the Pastoral Epistles. In Chapter 14 of Connolly's edition (or III, 1 in Funk's) we read:

Appoint as a widow one that is not under fifty years old, who in some sort, by reason of her years, shall be remote from the suspicion of taking a second husband. . . . But let not young widows be appointed to the widows' order: yet let them be taken care of and helped, lest by reason of their being in want they be minded to marry a second time, and some harmful matter ensue. For this you know, that she who marries one husband may lawfully marry also a second; but she who goes beyond this is a harlot.

Both groups were to receive support from the church. The procedure is clearly defined. Donors did not give directly to widows but rather to the bishop who distributed gifts to the widows at his discretion. On receiving an alms from the bishop, the widow was told the name of the giver in order to pray for him.[22] Besides praying for benefactors and for the whole church, widows were to make garments at home in order to provide for those in distress.[23] Further, they were to fast and pray for sick and distressed church members; they were to visit them and, what is most remarkable, they were to lay their hands on them.[24]

On the other hand, certain ministries were forbidden to widows and all women because they were women. The first was baptism:

That a woman should baptize, or that one should be baptized by a woman, we do not counsel, for it is a transgression of the commandment, and a great peril to her that baptizes and to him who is baptized. For if it were lawful to be baptized by a woman, our Lord and Teacher Himself would have been baptized by Mary His mother, whereas He was baptized by John, like others of the people. Do not therefore imperil yourselves, brethren and sisters, by acting beside the law of the Gospel.[25]

The second was teaching.

It is neither right nor necessary therefore that women should be teachers, and especially concerning the name of Christ and the redemption of His passion. For you have not been appointed to this, O women, and especially widows, that you should teach but that you should pray and entreat the Lord God. For He the Lord God, Jesus Christ our Teacher, sent us the Twelve to instruct the People and the Gentiles; and there were with us women disciples, Mary Magdalene and Mary the daughter of James and the other Mary; but He did not send them to instruct the people with us. For if it were required that women should teach, our Master Himself would have commanded these to give instruction with us.[26]

In both instances the reasons for forbidding these ministries to women were found in our Lord's example rather than in St. Paul's.

Concerning deaconesses, this work also has much to say. Indeed, it furnishes the only major reference to deaconesses in all the extra-canonical literature of the Ante-Nicene period, and its conception of the female diaconate is a lofty one. In an analogy between the Christian ministry and the Trinity the deaconess is likened to the Holy Spirit:

. . . for the bishop sits for you in the place of God Almighty. But the deacon stands in the place of Christ; and you do love him. And the deaconess shall be honoured by you in the place of the Holy Spirit; and the presbyters shall be to you in the likeness of the Apostles; and the orphans and widows shall be reckoned by you in the likeness of the altar.[27]

In a unique passage concerning the appointment and duties of deaconesses the *Didascalia* declares:

Wherefore, O bishop, appoint thee workers of righteousness as helpers who may co-operate with thee unto salvation. Those that please thee out of all the people thou shalt choose and appoint as deacons: a man for the performance of the most things that are required, but a woman for the ministry of women. For there are houses whither thou canst not send a deacon to the women, on account of the heathen, but mayest send a deaconess. Also, because in many other matters the office of a woman deacon is required. In the first place, when women go down into the water, those who go down into the water ought to be anointed by a deaconess with the oil of anointing; and where there is no woman at hand, and especially no deaconess, he who baptizes must of necessity anoint her who is being baptized. But where there is a woman, and especially a deaconess, it is not fitting that women should be seen by men: but with the imposition of hand do thou anoint the head only. As of old the priests and kings were anointed in Israel, do thou in like manner, with the imposition of hand, anoint the head of those who receive baptism, whether of men or of women; and afterwards—whether thou thyself baptize, or thou command the deacons or presbyters to baptize—let a woman deacon, as we have already said, anoint the women. But let a man pronounce over them the invocation of the divine Names in the water.

And when she who is being baptized has come up from the water, let the deaconess receive her, and teach and instruct her how the seal of baptism ought to be kept unbroken in purity and holiness. For this cause we say that the ministry of a woman deacon is especially needful and important. For our Lord and Saviour also was ministered unto by women ministers, Mary Magdalene, and Mary the daughter of James and mother of Jose, and the mother of the sons of Zebedee, with other women beside. And thou also hast need of the ministry of a deaconess for many things; for a deaconess is required to go into the houses of the heathen where there are believing women, and to visit those who are sick, and to minister to them in that of which they have need, and to bathe those who have begun to recover from sickness.[28]

The necessity for deaconesses and their ministry is quite clear from the passage. One needs only to make two observations. (1) Even deaconesses came under the earlier prohibition to women concerning the performance of baptism. The actual performance of the rite was to be done by men. The prohibition against teaching, however, was modified at least to the extent that deaconesses should teach other women the responsibilities of the Christian life. (2) The ministration of women was based upon the similar ministry of women during the life of Christ.

CONCLUSIONS

From the present consideration of the three Church Orders which belong to the third century representing Christian life and order in both the East and the West, certain conclusions may be drawn. Without question these documents show that widows were the most prominent group of women in the church. The ministry of prayer was universally assigned to them. In addition they were delegated certain ministries in relation to the sick. Clearly there were enrolled widows and those who were not. Support for them came regularly from the church, but no liturgical ministry was allowed widows.

Virgins were a minor group according to these documents. They were certainly not an order in any sense of the word nor was there any special merit attached to the state of virginity.

It is, however, the detailed word concerning deaconesses in the *Didascalia* which is the most extraordinary feature of these writings. They appear as a well-established and well-recognized group with specific ministries to perform in the church. In all other Ante-Nicene literature there are only slight and relatively insignificant references to deaconesses. How does one account for the suddenness of their appearance in the *Didascalia* as a well-developed group after the silence of the preceding years? The usual answer is to say as Cecilia Robinson does: "There was no continuous existence of the female diaconate in the strict sense, but in the third century the needs of the church called for a revival of the office." [29] However, such an answer practically assumes that deaconesses in the third century had the same functions as in New Testament times. One feels that this is reading back into the New Testament much of the development which had clearly taken place in the office and ministry of deaconesses as they appear in the Church Orders. Rather than the word *revival* one would suggest the word *development* to describe what happened.

If this be a development, is it possible to trace any intermediate steps between the simple picture in the New Testament of women's ministry and the well-developed picture in the *Didascalia* of the female diaconate? This is a most difficult question because there is so little clear evidence, but one ventures to suggest the following. It will be recalled that the *Apostolic Church Order* divided praying widows from nursing widows. Further, the *Didascalia* assigned to deaconesses a similar ministry to that of the nursing widows of the *Apostolic Church Order*. The *Didascalia* stated that widows also had nursing duties. In other words, a part of the ministry of deaconesses overlaps that of widows. Possibly then that intermediate step between the New Testament and the *Didascalia* was simply this: as the order of widows grew in numbers and importance the ministry of widows began to expand from that of intercession to include that of ministering to the sick. The usefulness and advisability of this impressed the church and its leaders until at length certain widows were definitely set aside for this service. Such a widow would naturally be called *hē diakonos*. It is not difficult to see how other duties would have been added to her ministry in time. This explanation accounts for all the existing evidence, and is confirmed by a regulation in the fourth century *Apostolic Constitutions* which says: "But let a Deaconess be a pure virgin; but if not, then a widow once married, faithful and honourable." [30] This indicates that deaconesses at that time were chosen from one of the recognized groups in the church, and lends support to the suggestion put forth that earlier they were chosen from the order of widows. Further light and more definite conclusions would require further evidence, but this seems to be the most plausible suggestion in the light of the evidence.

QUESTIONS

1. According to church orders, were women allowed to teach in the church during the third century?

2. How do deaconesses emerge as a distinct group during the third century?

NOTES

[1] James 2:1–9; 1:27; Hebrews 10:25; I Thessalonians 5:27; II Thessalonians 3:10–12.

[2] J. Armitage Robinson, "Deaconesses in the 'Apostolic Constitutions,'" *The Ministry of Women* (London, SPCK, 1919), p. 77.

[3] James Vernon Bartlet, *Church-Life and Church-Order* (Oxford, Basil Blackwell, 1943), p. 145.

[4] John Wordsworth, *The Ministry of Grace* (London, Longmans, Green & Co., 1901), p. 15.

[5] Bartlet, *op. cit.*, pp. 153–154.

[6] R. Hugh Connolly, *The So-Called Egyptian Church Order and Derived Documents* (Cambridge, Cambridge University Press, 1916), pp. 147–149.

[7] Gregory Dix, *The Treatise on the Apostolic Tradition of St. Hippolytus of Rome* (New York, Macmillan, 1937), p. xxxviii.

[8] *Ibid.*, pp. xxxix–xl.

[9] *Ibid.*, p. xliv.

[10] xi. 4.

[11] Cf. Eusebius, *Ecclesiastical History*, VI, 43.

[12] xxvii.

[13] xiii.

[14] xviii. 1.

[15] xviii. 5.

[16] xvi. 24.

[17] Adolf Harnack, *Sources of the Apostolic Canons* (London, 1895), pp. 2–6.

[18] Bartlet, *op. cit.*, pp. 102–103.

[19] Harnack, *op. cit.*, p. 20.

[20] Chaps. 27 and 28.

[21] R. Hugh Connolly, *Didascalia Apostolorum* (Oxford, Clarendon Press, 1929), pp. v and xci.

[22] Chap. 9 (II, 27). The reference in parenthesis is to Funk's edition; the other to Connolly's.

[23] Chap. 15 (III, 8).

[24] Chap. 15 (III, 7).

[25] Chap. 15 (III, 9).

[26] Chap. 15 (III, 6).

[27] Chap. 9 (II, 26).

[28] Chap. 16 (III, 12).

[29] *The Ministry of Deaconesses*, p. 84.

[30] VI, 17.

Chapter XIII

CONCLUSIONS

To summarize, systematize, and draw certain conclusions is my final task and the purpose of this chapter. There are gaps in the evidence which one would wish filled; nevertheless, we must state the facts which we do have and make conclusions and observations on that basis.

With regard to women, Christianity's inheritance from ancient Greece and Rome was small. In Greece, with the exception of Macedonia, women were without any doubt considered as inferiors and were kept in utter seclusion in the family. Stranger women, of course, had liberty, but the price of their liberty was harlotry. Legally, the Roman woman was little better off, but practically she did have much more freedom. However, this freedom brought with it widespread moral laxity; yet, rightly used it was a boon to Christian women who were active in the early days of the spread of Christianity throughout the Empire. There is no doubt that when the Christian message came, with its insistence on absolute purity, it brought protection to women and elevated their status. In some respects it is true that the Christian church worked within the framework of existing conditions, but in respect to its standards of purity for women "specifically Christian motives and sanctions are introduced." [1] The Apologists were persistent in their use of the higher standards of Christianity toward women as an important apologetic for the truth of the Christian message, and their very insistence underlines the uniqueness of this feature of that message.

The purity of marriage was the most important aspect of this higher standard. In a Christian civilization of the twentieth century it is easy to overlook how startling and important was the early church's insistence on the holiness and purity of marriage. Two distinctively Christian teachings contributed largely to this principle. One was Jesus' teaching concerning divorce, and the other was St. Paul's sacramental conception of marriage. This was a higher concept than was found in Judaism with its polygamy and allowance of divorce. Yet the idea of subordination of the woman to her husband which is so prominent in Judaism carries over with little change into the teaching of the church throughout the entire Ante-Nicean period. The reason for this is obvious. Believing in the divine inspiration of the Old Testament Scriptures and believing that the accounts of the Creation and Fall of man contained certain inalterable truths about subordination, New Testament writers did not even consider that there could be any change in the mind of God concerning the subordination of women. Thus they carried into the New Testament the idea that the special sphere of activity for women was in the home as the subordinate helpmeet yet co-ruler of the children.

In respect to divorce, however, the teaching of Christianity was different. It has been shown in this book that both Jesus and Paul taught that divorce has no place in the ideal Christian ethic, and this teaching was superior to the highest standards of contemporary Judaism. By whatever method Jesus' words are interpreted the result is the same—disallowance of divorce; and this was a distinct contribution of Christianity to the elevation of the status of women. In religious life, too, Christianity surpassed the teachings of Judaism, for, although in Judaism women were partakers of the covenant relationship, in Christianity they are one with men in Christ Jesus. Though women appeared frequently in the accounts of Israel's religious life, it was always in a secondary way; certainly they never played a part similar to that which Christian women played in the early expansion of the church. One important reason for this is simply that the unmarried Jewish woman was a reproach, while Christianity offered to the unmarried woman a sanctified service. The Founder Himself encouraged this idea by accepting the ministry of a number of women during His own earthly life.

Thus it is rightly said that Jesus was the turning point in the history of women, for He insisted on protecting the sanctity of their personal lives and promoting the activity of their religious lives.

Although it is abundantly clear that the Lord Jesus opened the doors of religious service to women by offering the first women who served Him something to do besides seeking remarriage, what lines of development this service took in the life of the church during the first three centuries has not always been easy to trace. However, certain conclusions can be stated.

In the early days of the expansion of the church, women ministered of their substance, hospitality, time, and labors in a significant and important way. Their role was important but it was not a leading one; that belonged to the men. From the very beginning there were many women converts, and this continued throughout the early period.[2] These converts were active, for the very quantity of material written concerning them witnesses to that fact. The regulations concerning women in the writings of Paul, Clement, Tertullian, and Cyprian indicate that they were playing an active part in the life of the church throughout the period. It is as obvious as pointing out that the Old Testament contains no chapters similar to I Corinthians 11 or 14.

The moving force behind all this was the Lord Himself, who turned the reproach of the unmarried or widowed Jewish woman into reputable service for the Master. The secondary force in promoting the activity of women was the developing strain of asceticism which tended to give priority to the unmarried woman and her service. Doubtless, too, the increasing prominence of widows gave impetus to asceticism among younger women. By Cyprian's time, at least, there was a large though unofficial group of virgins in the church. A third contributing factor to the increasing activity of women was the strong belief in the immediate second advent of the Lord.

Closely akin to this developing asceticism is the increasing prominence of virgins throughout these early centuries. The first mention is in Paul's word to them in I Corinthians 7. Though he clearly approved of their marrying, it is equally clear that he thought it preferable that they remain unmarried. At the beginning of the second century Polycarp directed that virgins' vows of chastity should be known only to the bishop. A hundred years later, Tertullian, who definitely gives preference to the celibate life, is also insistent on the maintenance of the private character of virgins' vows. Suddenly, however, in the writings of Cyprian virgins appear as a large and respected group in the church. Nevertheless, they had not developed into an order, although all the elements which would make up an order were present by the end of the third century. Thus the beginnings of virgins' orders were primitive and also primarily Western, at least in the Ante-Nicean period. Furthermore, there was no confusion between the virgin and widow throughout the period. One must recognize, too, that this ascetic spirit and prominence of virgins had an exalting effect on the status of women. The position and designations assigned to them by Cyprian all point to this conclusion; and certainly their rise in importance in Cyprian's time, so that they began to be a separate and distinguishable group within the congregation, elevated the status of women. Burkitt put it well when he wrote: "We must never forget that Christian asceticism has generally tended toward the equalization of the sexes. The historical opposite to the ascetic ideal was not that in which woman was looked upon as the divinely ordained household drudge or the plaything of man." [3]

As for the public ministry of women, we have shown that the general practice of New Testament churches was that women should keep silent in the church, and this practice continued without much variation throughout the first three centuries. Although the right of women to prophesy in private was exercised (as in the cases of Philip's daughters and Priscilla), it was excluded from the public gatherings of the church. Even in that Montanist assembly the visions that one woman had were reported to the male leaders of the church after the conclusion of the service. References in all the literature to itinerant prophets is always to male ones. Thus clearly the direction and exercise of public worship was in the hands of men.

This does not mean, of course, that women had no responsibility in the life of the church. Something of the extent of their activity in the expansion of the church has already been reviewed. It now remains to summarize what the evidence has shown about their position in the official life of the Christian community.

Beyond any question the widow was the outstanding figure throughout the entire first three centuries of the church. Although Jewish widows did seek remarriage, the degeneration of the use of the *leviratus* meant that they had to be supported from a fund in the temple, and the young Christian community could do and did do no less for widows whom it numbered among its converts. However, Christianity did more than Judaism by offering to its widows who resolved not to remarry the privilege of consecrated spiritual service. "This state of widowhood was new." [4] What service these widows may have performed for the church in its very beginning is not known, but it is not impossible to conceive of their being active in a similar manner to those women who ministered to Jesus. Nevertheless, one must not assume too much, for the emphasis in all the early writings is on the service the church rendered to them, and not vice versa. Ignatius spoke of their dedicated character, while Polycarp definitely indicated (as did Paul in the Pastorals) that their ministry was that of intercession. The Pastorals indicated that there was an enrolled group of widows very early whose support was officially assumed by the church. Evidently official duties were not prerequisite to official enrolling, though the ministry of prayer was expected of all widows. Possibly, too, they served the church by helping to rear orphan children. In some ways it would seem quite proper to call this group a diaconate of widows.[5] But whatever their actual service may or may not have been, it is important to emphasize that the very drawing up of ecclesiastical regulations for women in these very early days "was quite a unique creation of the church," [6] and it did elevate and sanctify the status of women in the church.

Although in the first and early part of the second centuries widows may have performed various duties for the church not because they were officially commissioned to do so but simply because they were women, as the order of widows became more definitely established no ministry except that of prayer is mentioned in connection with widows. In Rome, according to the *Apostolic Tradition,* widows had no active ministry at the beginning of the third century. This is confirmed by the letter of Pope Cornelius written in the middle of the same century. In other words, whatever ministry widows may have performed at the very beginning was not performed because they were widows but simply because they were women. The development and defining of the order was not for the purpose that widows might become an order of ministers but the object of ministry by the church. One outstanding exception to this general statement was found in the Egyptian church where, as witnessed by the third century *Apostolic Church Order,* there was a division among the widows into those who ministered in prayer and those who ministered in sickness and visitation. A suggestion as to what this means will be made below. Widows, then, were beyond all doubt the most outstanding and universally recognized group of women in the life of the church during this early period.

The origin and development of the office of deaconess is a much more difficult and involved matter simply because there is so little evidence. The early church recognized clearly the need for women workers, and there is no doubt that women "deaconed" in the general sense of the term. Phoebe, the only woman actually called a deaconess in the New Testament, must have had a place of leadership in the church at Cenchrea, though it does not seem advisable to conclude that this leadership was anything more than acting as patroness of that church. It cannot be proved that it included rulership nor is it proof that an official female diaconate existed in those days. Even Miss Robinson, who would be prone to try to use Phoebe to prove the existence of official deaconesses, declares: "We are, however, hardly justified in assuming that S. Paul uses the word here in a strictly official sense." [7] With that I heartily agree. I find it difficult also to assume that the mention of the women in I Timothy 3:11 refers to deaconesses in the official sense. Rather, it seems to refer to deacons' wives, and yet it does bear evidence to the fact that women did assist in ministering, especially in visitation. It could hardly be more than that sort of ministry since deacons themselves had not been assigned a spiritual ministry that early in the history of the church. Neither does the evidence of Pliny's letter warrant the conclusion that deaconesses were an official order in the church in either the first or second century.

However, in the third century document, the *Didascalia,* deaconesses appear suddenly as a well-established and well-recognized group with specific ministries. These duties were not liturgical but consisted of helping at baptisms and visiting the sick. Such ministry was justified by the fact that women ministered to the Lord during His lifetime, although the *Didascalia* does not suggest that the type of ministry was the same. In other words, one must not read back into the New Testament a development which came later and which is clear only in the third century.

What, then, does the silence of the first two centuries and the development in the office of deaconess mean? I suggest this. Though the ministry of women in the early church was limited in its scope, it was not limited to any particular group of women. Doubtless there were widows among the group who ministered to Jesus. Phoebe herself may have been a widow. Perhaps the younger widows who went from house to house did so in the discharge of some duty for the church.[8] At Ephesus the wives of deacons helped their husbands in their ministry of visitation. Paul indicates in I Corinthians 7 that virgins served the Lord in a way that might be called "deaconing." As time went on, however, though there was never any confusion between the groups, the particular distinctiveness of widows, virgins, and deaconesses developed. Virgins became prominent in the West; widows appeared everywhere; and deaconesses appeared as a fully developed group in the East, but a group whose development seems to come in a broken and indirect line from the early church. Why is this so? Possibly it is because as the other groups of women developed their own distinctive ministries and characteristics, a gap was left in the performance of certain necessary ministries. The large and respected group of virgins in the West had no particular ministry assigned to them. Widows were limited to the ministry of intercession. Who, then, would do the work of visitation and dispensing of relief which widows, virgins, and deacons' wives all did in the very first days of the church?

Not only was there a need for deaconesses, but there were also examples of serving women in the days of Christ and there were examples of deacons both of which probably served as patterns in the developing of the order of deaconesses. Certain women had to be given official duties, and these became deaconesses in the official sense. I have suggested, on the basis of the evidence of the *Apostolic Church Order* and the *Didascalia*, that in some cases at least the deaconesses of the third century, who are really the first official deaconesses for whom there is conclusive evidence, were appointed from among the widows. This may not have happened in every case or in every place, but all the evidence points to the fact that deaconesses did not constitute anything like an official group until the third century. The evidence also indicates that the order developed as a result of the development and defining of the order of widows and not as a natural outgrowth of the privilege of serving which women exercised in the earliest days of the church. The direct ancestors of the deaconesses, then, were not the ministering women of Christ's day, or Phoebe, or the deacons' wives at Ephesus, but the widows as they developed into a definite order. The development of deaconesses into an official group came in an indirect and broken line from the days of the New Testament.

In all of this discussion one must not lose sight of the fact that throughout this period the place of women in the home was really that which the church emphasized. Some writers had to devote much space to women's religious activities because of the problems involved, but that does not mean that Christianity was not concerned with the home. Not only did the church protect the rights of her women, but Christian love and all the relationships of a Christian home are conceived of in the very highest way. The Christian church clearly believed and taught subordination (but not inferiority), and it was through this very subordination that honor and responsibility came to women. This was her sphere, and neither the ascetic trend nor the increased religious activity supersede the prominence and honor given to a woman in the home.

This is the evidence concerning the status of women in the early church, and these are the conclusions which can be based on it. Many desired things are lacking in the evidence and in the final picture, but since all the evidence has been presented, one must be content with the conclusions. One more question must be asked. In Donaldson's words it is this: "What is the ideal of woman? What could we call the complete development and full blossoming of woman's life?" [9] It is a question which is much agitated in all branches of the Christian church today, and it is a question which has presented itself again and again as this study was being made. Those who share this author's view of inspiration will answer it by saying that in the inspired writings we have the mind of God concerning the full development of women. And this will mean subordination and honor in the home, silence and helpfulness in the church, according to the teaching and pattern of the New Testament. At least that ought to be the answer of all who believe in the divine inspiration and authority of the Scriptures, for if these teachings concerning women are not authoritative then what teachings in the New Testament are? Those who do not share such a view of inspiration will still have to face the problem of whether or not the early church thought that its conception of the status of women was ideal and included woman's full development. Each one must also decide to what extent his answer will influence his opinion about these matters in the twentieth century. But for all it is a question which "it is requisite for the historian of woman in any age to put . . . to himself and his readers." [10] Thus we ask it, and with our asking we have presented that on which the answer must be based—the evidence concerning the place of women in the early church.

QUESTIONS

1. Does the Old Testament emphasize the place of women in the home or in worship?

2. What is the inspired picture concerning the place of women as revealed in the New Testament?

3. Do you think that this picture represents the ideal for women today?

4. If the New Testament is authoritative for us today, then what should women be doing in order to fulfill their God-given place in the Christian community?

NOTES

[1] C. H. Dodd, *Gospel and Law* (New York, Columbia University Press, 1951), p. 24.

[2] Cf. the decrees during the persecution of Licinius (A.D. 307): (1) men and women could not worship together; (2) women were not to enter places of worship; (3) women were to be taught religion by women only and not by bishops. These seem to indicate that the emperor considered that one of the strongholds of Christianity was its women (Eusebius, *Life of Constantine*, I, liii).

[3] F. Crawford Burkitt, *The Gospel History and Its Transmission* (Edinburgh, T. & T. Clark, 1906), pp. 214–215.

[4] Joseph Viteau, "L'Institution des Diacres et des Veuves," *Revue d'Histoire Ecclésiastique*, XXII (1926), 530.

[5] As Viteau, *loc. cit.*

[6] Harnack, *The Mission and Expansion of Christianity in the First Three Centuries* (London: Williams & Norgate, 1908), II, 72.

[7] Cecilia Robinson, *The Ministry of Deaconesses* (London: Methuen & Co., 1898), p. 10.

[8] I Timothy 5:13.

[9] *Woman* . . . , pp. 1–2.

[10] *Ibid.*, p. 2.

SUBJECT INDEX

Adam, 79
Alexander the Great, 4
Angels, 31, 74
Anna, 12
Annunciation, 20
Aphrodite, 59-60
Apollos, 55
Apphia, 56
Aristotle, 2
Asceticism, 63, 102, 117, 140, 141, 145
Athens, 2-4, 54

Bacchus, worship of, 7
Baptism, 70-71, 120, 132-133, 135
Bishops, 97, 98, 114, 117, 123, 128, 130, 133, 134, 141, 147

Celibacy, 62-64, 85, 101, 102, 103-104, 105, 108, 111, 117, 123, 131, 135, 140-141
Chloe, 89
Christ
  and Mary, 21-23
  annunciation, 20
  anointed, 31
  crucifixion, 36
  genealogies, 19-20
  headship, 68
  resurrection, 36-38
  second advent, 63, 117, 140
Church
  deaconesses in, 85-91
  in homes, 55
  widows in, 81-85, 118, 122, 128, 130-131, 135
  women in, 71-81, 117, 119-121, 122, 141, 147

Circumcision, 70
City-State, 2-4
Concubinage, 9
Corinth, 59-60
Council of Trent, 43

Damaris, 54
Deacon, 86, 97, 100, 128, 130, 134
Deaconess, 85-91
  Apostolic Constitutions, 136
  Apostolic Fathers, 100-101, 103
  Apostolic Tradition, 129
  Clement of Alexandria, 109
  Didascalia, 133-136, 144
  Ignatius, 98
  Origen, 111
  Phoebe, 85, 86-90, 91, 111, 143, 144, 145
  Pliny, 85, 102-103, 144
  summary statement, 143-145
Deborah, 12
Demosthenes, 4
Disciples, 31, 34, 36-37, 56
Divorce
  Christ and, 40-49, 62, 139
  in Judaism, 10, 40-41
  in Rome, 6, 43
  Paul and, 64-65
  Roman Catholic view, 43
Docetism, 98
Dorcas, 81-82

Education, 9, 27-30
Esther, 9
Eunice, 9, 10
Euodia, 54, 56
Eve, 12, 79, 116

Fall of man, 79, 111, 116, 129, 139

Genealogies, 19-20
Great commission, 31

Hagar, 12
Hannah, 9, 11
Headship
of Christ, 68
of man, 74, 110, 117
Heathen, status of women among, 101-102, 116-117
Hetairai, 4
Home
Christian, 66-68, 98, 107, 117, 139, 145
Greek, 3
Jewish, 13
Roman, 5
Huldah, 12

Joanna, 35, 36
Junia, 56

Leah, 9
Lois, 9, 10
Lydia, 54

Macedonia, 4-5, 54
Manoah's wife, 9
Mark, 10
Marriage, 48, 59-65, 102, 104, 105, 108, 116, 138-139
Mary (Magdalene), 35, 133, 134
Mary (mother of Jesus), 19-24, 35, 132
Mary (mother of John Mark), 54
Mary (Rom. 16:6), 55, 56
Maximilla, 115
Miriam, 12
Mohammedanism, 8
Montanism, 113, 114-115, 141
Motherhood, 3, 9-10, 13, 21, 23

Naomi, 9
Nazarite, 12
Noadiah, 12
Nymphas, 58

Oppius, 5
Orphans, 84, 103

Peninnah, 11
Philip's daughters, 32, 141
Phoebe, 85, 86-90, 91, 111, 143, **144,** 145
Plato, 2
Prayer
of widows, 83-84, 100, 118, 128, 131, 135, 142-143
of women in church, 77-81
Priscilla, 9, 55, 56, 57, 115, **141**
Prophecy, 73, 114, 115, 141
Prophets, 97, 114, 141

Rachel, 9
Rahab, 20
Rebekah, 9
Resurrection, 29-30, 36-38
Rufus's mother, 56
Ruth, 9, 20

Salome, 35, 36
Samson's mother, 12
Sarah, 12, 67
Seneca, 6
Silence of women in church, 72, **74-** 81
Slavery, 9, 11, 129
Sparta, 2
Stoicism, 7
Subordination, 66-67, 71, 72-74, **108,** 111, 116, 139, 145
Supper, Lord's, 31, 54
Susanna, 35, 36
Synagogue, 7-8, 12-13, 87-88
Syntyche, 54, 56

Tamar, 20
Thekla, 104, 120
Thucydides, 4
Tongues, 74, 75

Veil, 72-74, 78, 109, 115, 116, **117,** 129
Virgins, teaching concerning
Apostolic Fathers, 103
Apostolic Tradition, 128-129
Cyprian, 65, 122-124, 140, **141**
Didascalia, 131, 135
Ignatius, 99
Paul, 65
Tertullian, 115, 116, 117, **118-119**

Widows, teaching concerning
  Apostolic Church Order, 130-131,
    136
  Apostolic Fathers, 103
  Apostolic Tradition, 128
  Clement of Alexandria, 109
  Cyprian, 122
  Didascalia, 132-133, 135
  Ignatius, 99
  in Acts, 81-82, 86
  in time of Christ, 35
  Lucian, 103
  Paul, 83-85
  summary statement, 142-143
  Tertullian, 118-119

Zebedee, 10

SCRIPTURE INDEX

GENESIS

1:26	74
2.24	48
3:13 ff.	12
3:16	79
16:8 ff.	12
18:9, 15	12
21:17 ff.	12

EXODUS

15:20	12
19:11	11
20:12	10
21:7–11	9
21:15, 17	10
22:22, 24	11

LEVITICUS

6:29	12
10:14	12
12	12
12:2, 5	9
15:19–33	12
19:3	10

NUMBERS

5:11–31	21
6:2	12
12:2	12

DEUTERONOMY

5:16	10
12:12, 18	11
14:26	11
16:11–14	11
22:13–30	11
24:1	10, 40, 41
24:19	81

25:7–10	81
26:12–13	81
27:19	81

JUDGES

4:4	12
11:40	12
13:3 ff.	12
13:20	12
21:6–25	11

RUTH

4:4–10	81

I SAMUEL

1:1 ff.	11
2:19 ff.	11

II SAMUEL

6:19	11

II KINGS

22:13–20	12

II CHRONICLES

35:25	12

EZRA

2:65	12

NEHEMIAH

6:14	12
7:67	12
12:43	12

PSALMS

23:5	33
45:14	13
68:5	81

68:24–25	12
138:1	74

PROVERBS

1:8	10
6:20	10
20:20	10
23:22	10
28:24	10
30:11, 17	10
31	82
31:10, 25–28	8

ISAIAH

8:3	12
50:1	10

JEREMIAH

3:8	10
16:7	12

MICAH

6:4	12

MALACHI

2:16	10

MATTHEW

1:1–17	19
1:3, 5–6	20
1:19	20, 47
1:20	21
4:11	34
5	44
5:21–24	44
5:27–28	44
5:31–32	41
5:32	43
6:2–4	82
6:28	28
8:15	34
9:20–22	27
10:37	22
12:50	26
13:2	28
14:21	27
15:19	47
15:21–28	27
19	44
19:3	41
19:3–9	41, 45
19:9	43
19:10	41

22:30	31
24:40–41	28
27:55	34, 35
27:56	36
28:1	36
28:7	36
28:16–20	31

MARK

1:13	34
1:31	34
3:31–35	22
3:35	26
5:25–34	27
7:25–30	27
10	42, 44
10:2–12	41, 45
10:29	22
12:25	31, 63
12:40	35
12:41–44	30
13:17	62
15:40	36
15:41	34, 35
16:1	36
16:7	36
16:11, 14	36

LUKE

1:28	20
2:36	12
2:41–52	21
3:23–38	19
4:16, 20	12
4:39	34
7:36–50	31
8:2–3	35
8:3	34, 35, 36
8:21	26
8:43–48	27
8:47	31
10:1	31
10:38–42	29
10:40	34
11:5–8	28
11:27–28	22
12:53	27
13:10–17	30
13:18–21	28
16:18	41, 45
18:1–5	28
20:35–36	31

20:47   35
21:1–4   30
23:49   36
23:55–56   36
24:1   36
24:9   36
24:10   36

JOHN
2:1–12   22
2:4   22
4   32, 36
4:1–42   92
4:21   22
8:2–11   30
11:1–44   30
12:1–11   31
12:2   34
12:6   35
19:25   22, 35, 36
19:26   22
20:1   36
20:17   36
20:19–23   31

ACTS
1:14   24
1:15   53
2:17–18   73
4:4   57
5:14   53
6:1–7   81, 86
6:2   85
8:3   54
8:12–17   54
9:36   39
9:36–41   81
11:27–30   114
12:12   54
13:14 ff.   12
15:29   47
16:14   54
16:16, 19   54
16:40   54
17:4, 12   54
17:34   54
18:2, 26   55
18:26   55
20:24   85
21:9   73

ROMANS
10:12   70

12:8   87
13:14   86
16   55-56
16:1   85
16:1-2   111
16:3   55

I CORINTHIANS
1:7   73
3:5   85
5:1   47
6:12–14   60
7   59, 60, 109, 140, 144
7:2   61
7:2, 28   60
7:5   61
7:7, 8, 27, 29, 32, 33, 38, 40   62
7:10   64-65
7:11   46, 50
7:26   60
7:29–31   63
7:32, 34   64
7:32–35   63
7:36–38   65
7:39   65
9:5   109
11   75, 76, 77, 140
11:3–5   72
11:5   77, 78, 91, 93
11:10   74
11:11   74
11:15   74
11:15–18   72
11:16   74
12:13   70
12:28   114
14   75, 76, 77, 140
14:34   75, 79, 91, 93
14:34–35   72, 122
14:35   75
15:5   37
15:5-7   36
15:6   37
16:15   85
16:19   55

GALATIANS
2:17   86
3:19   74
3:26-28   70
3:28   26

EPHESIANS
1:6   20
3:7   85
4:11   114
5   66, 109
5:22-23   59
5:25   66
6:1   21

PHILIPPIANS
1:1   86
4:2   54
4:3   54

COLOSSIANS
1:7   85, 86
3   109
3:11   70
4:15   58
4:17   85

I THESSALONIANS
5:12   87
5:27   126

II THESSALONIANS
3:10-12   126

I TIMOTHY
2   76
2:8-9   76
2:11-14   122
2:12   72, 75, 76,
                78

2:13   79
2:13-14   79
2:14   79
3:4, 5, 12   87
3:8-10   86
3:11   85, 90,
                143
4:6   85, 86
5:3   83
5:3-16   82
5:4, 16   82
5:5   83
5:9   82
5:10   84, 99
5:13   84, 133
5:14   85
5:17   87

II TIMOTHY
4:5   85
4:19   55

TITUS
2   123
3:8, 14   87

HEBREWS
10:25   126

JAMES
1:27   126
2:1-9   126

I PETER
1:12   74
3   66
3:1-7   59
3:7   66

Moody Press, a ministry of the Moody Bible Institute, is
designed for education, evangelization and edification.
If we may assist you in knowing more about Christ and
the Christian life, please write us without obligation to:
Moody Press, c/o MLM, Chicago, Illinois 60610.